Praise for *No Act of Love Is Ever Wasted*

Bold, powerful, and compelling. Truly a landmark book, *No Act of Love Is Ever Wasted* is full of profound insight and practical wisdom. Morgan and Thibault provide a thoughtful and compassionate look at issues of enormous relevance to persons concerned about and struggling with dementia, as well as to family members, caregivers, pastors, and community members.

—Dr. RICHARD H. GENTZLER JR.
Director, Center on Aging & Older Adult Ministries
General Board of Discipleship, The United Methodist Church

Jane Thibault and Richard Morgan open our eyes to the spiritual options of dealing with everyone affected by dementia. This book puts a new, restorative option into caring for persons with dementia and their caregivers. It tells where God fits into this equation and helps each of us rethink our path in this process.

—LOUIS W. CATALANO JR., MD
Neurologist and Director
The Neurological Institute of Western Pennsylvania

What a wonderful gift Jane Thibault and Richard Morgan offer caregivers. They remind us of the abiding worth of every person and the enduring power of even the smallest act of love. Biblically grounded and rich in practical suggestions, this book will bring comfort and hope to all those caring for loved ones with dementia.

—KATHLEEN FISCHER, PhD, MSW
Author of *Winter Grace: Spirituality and Aging*
Psychotherapist and spiritual director
Seattle, Washington

I absolutely affirm the message of assurance presented in *No Act of Love Is Ever Wasted*. Anyone who knows and loves a person with dementia will benefit from the experiences, insights, and recommendations that Jane and Richard have shared in this dynamic look at caring about, and for, the spirituality of people who have dementia.

—DENTON C. HARTMAN, MS, NHA
Former Director of Dementia Services
Menno Haven Retirement Communities
Chambersburg, Pennsylvania

As I read this book, I was moved by the amount of caring and love the authors conveyed. Their rich understanding of dementia and the journey caregivers endure is evident throughout the text. The perspective that caregiving is an extension of spiritual life will aid families and professionals to look beyond day-to-day routines and chores and see their role as an opportunity to serve the total person in body, mind, and spirit.

—LOIS W. LUTZ, MS
Alzheimer Education and Outreach Coordinator
Pittsburgh, Pennsylvania

No Act of Love Is Ever Wasted is a rich resource for care providers, clergy, and staff of residential care facilities. It asks difficult questions but also breaks new ground in sharing many examples of people with dementia who evidence the deep emotional and spiritual expression that is possible when someone will listen and be present to them.

—ELIZABETH MACKINLAY, AM, PHD
Director, Centre for Ageing and Pastoral Studies
School of Theology, Charles Sturt University
Canberra, Australia

NO ACT OF LOVE IS EVER WASTED

The Spirituality of Caring for Persons with Dementia

JANE MARIE THIBAULT, PhD

RICHARD L. MORGAN, PhD

UPPER ROOM BOOKS®
NASHVILLE

NO ACT OF LOVE IS EVER WASTED:
The Spirituality of Caring for Persons with Dementia
Copyright © 2009 by Jane Marie Thibault and Richard L. Morgan
All rights reserved.

The Upper Room Web site: www.upperroom.org

UPPER ROOM®, UPPER ROOM BOOKS®, and design logos are trademarks owned by The Upper Room®, a ministry of GBOD®, Nashville, Tennessee. All rights reserved.

At the time of publication, all Web sites referenced in this book were valid. However, due to the fluid nature of the Internet, some addresses may have changed or the content may no longer be relevant.

The publisher gratefully acknowledges permission from the author to reprint "They Will Remember," excerpted from the poem "This Is (to) Mary Margaret Yearwood" by James Fowler. The poem appeared in *In Their Hearts: Inspirational Alzheimer's Stories* by Mary Margaret Britton Yearwood (Victoria, BC: Trafford Publishing, 2002), 147–48.

Unless otherwise indicated, scripture quotations are from the New Revised Standard Version Bible, copyright 1989, Division of Christian Education of the National Council of the Churches of Christ in the United States of America. Used by permission. All rights reserved.

Scriptures marked KJV are from the King James Version.

Cover image: Photos.com
Cover design: Jeff Miller, The DesignWorks Group
Interior design: Buckinghorse Design / www.buckinghorsedesign.com
First printing: 2009

Library of Congress Cataloging-in-Publication Data
Thibault, Jane M. (Jane Marie), 1946–
No act of love is ever wasted : the spirituality of caring for persons with dementia / Jane Marie Thibault and Richard L. Morgan.
      p. cm.
Includes bibliographical references.
ISBN 978-0-8358-9995-6
1. Caregivers—Religious life. 2. Caring—Religious aspects—Christianity.
3. Dementia. I. Morgan, Richard Lyon, 1929– II. Title.
  BV4910.9.T45 2009
  259'.42—dc22

                          2008055867

Printed in the United States of America

To the quiet majority of caregivers
who perform unimaginable acts of love
to provide quality care
for their loved ones

and

to our spouses,
Ron Fryrear and Alice Ann Morgan,
for their loving support

Dear Reader,

Cowriting this book has been both a challenge (Richard is in Pittsburgh, and Jane is in Louisville) and a great joy (our friendship has flourished). Both of us bring to this book our years of varied experience in caring for persons with dementia and working with their families. Throughout the book we will alternate "speaking." So that you will not be confused about who is talking, we will identify ourselves as (Richard) or (Jane) or merely say "we."

All of the names in the stories in this book have been changed to preserve confidentiality. They are real stories about real persons suffering from a dementing disease.

—Dick and Jane

CONTENTS

THEY WILL REMEMBER

In those places of the heart,
where soul still lurks,
they will remember.
In tactile hunger for hands that caress and care,
they will remember.
. . . .
At heaven's gate
where all the leaves
of lost memories are restored,
they WILL remember
all the loving fragments, melodies, touches,
prayers and tales by which you loved them.
Angels will sing, dance and shout,
sensing your love in these loved ones' joys.

—Jim Fowler

FOREWORD

After reading this magnificent book, I had a flash-back to the early 1960s, when a few of us clergy became involved in thanatology, the scientific study of death and dying. Many colleagues greeted me with suspicion and derision, making comments like these: "Why bother studying this topic? Didn't your theology classes, study of liturgy, and discussion on counseling the bereaved prepare you enough for dealing with death? If survivors still have difficulties, refer them to a psychiatrist."

Thankfully, much has changed since then. Seminaries introduced clinical pastoral education (CPE) programs, as well as seminars on death and dying. At last these institutions recognized that when their students explored loss in all its dimensions, they would be able to bring a more complete measure of healing to their congregants who were in the throes of lingering pain and suffering.

Authors Jane Thibault and Richard Morgan remind us that for some people, brain disease is a "taboo subject." They lament that clergy are seldom present with persons who have dementia unless death is imminent, and few theological schools offer training in how to minister to those with dementia.

We pastors have witnessed those heartbreaking, traumatic moments when our own family members, friends, and congregational members slowly descend into dementia. We anxiously watch the dwindling impairment of their mental activity, sense of meaning, understanding, judgment, and mood, as well as the decline of their physical abilities. We desperately want to help, but what can we do? We may feel unprepared, uncomfortable, and vulnerable as we are reminded of our own mortality.

We may try to excuse ourselves from contact with persons in mental decline by saying these people will forget our visits. . . . But we must not absolve ourselves of responsibility.

Thibault and Morgan report that by age eighty-five, more than half of us are susceptible to some form of dementia. This fact is even scarier, given that research has not found a cure, nor is one in sight.

We may try to excuse ourselves from contact with persons in mental decline by saying these people will probably forget our visits. We may even think there is nothing we can do. But we must not absolve ourselves of responsibility by leaving their care to professionals.

The pages of this thoughtfully researched and groundbreaking book present practical advice for caregivers and clergy. The person with dementia asks together with the caregiver: "Why me?" "Why us?" "Where is God in this situation?" Dr. Thibault and Dr. Morgan emphasize that "loving a person with dementia is a unique, mutual spiritual path. . . . We learn to love generously without constraint, without praise or thanks, sometimes despite a slap in the face."

This is a must book for caregivers, clergy, seminary students, and anyone concerned with spiritual care. The authors offer their own experiences, clinical examples, spiritual readings, questions to ponder, and astute suggestions for leading a support group for persons with dementia. They make compelling connections with religion, psychology, history, and philosophy.

Thibault and Morgan take us deeply into the realm of human torment. Yet their essential message is one of hope as they help us behold the human spirit's capacity to transform tragedy into healing, growth, and triumphant living. *No Act of Love Is Ever Wasted* is a gem to be treasured—to be read, discussed, and acted upon.

I like how the Reverend Richard Morgan concludes worship services for persons with dementia—by telling each individual "Namaste," or "The God in me greets the God in you."

—Dr. Earl A. Grollman, DHL, DD
Coauthor, *When Someone You Love Has Alzheimer's:*
The Caregiver's Journey

Introduction

NEEDED: LIVING WATER

> Jesus, tired out by his journey, was sitting by the well. It was about noon.
>
> A Samaritan woman came to draw water, and Jesus said to her, "Give me a drink." . . . The Samaritan woman said to him, "How is it that you, a Jew, ask a drink of me, a woman of Samaria?" . . . Jesus answered her, "If you knew the gift of God, and who it is that is saying to you, 'Give me a drink,' you would have asked him, and he would have given you living water. . . . Everyone who drinks of this water will be thirsty again, but those who drink of the water that I will give them will never be thirsty. The water that I will give will become in them a spring of water gushing up to eternal life."
>
> —John 4:6-14

Jim lingered at the end of our Sunday school class. He had told me (Richard) about the stress he had undergone while caring for loved ones with dementia. We sat for over an hour, skipping the worship service, as Jim vented his feelings. Both of his parents had suffered from Alzheimer's disease.

"I lost my father after a long struggle with this disease," he said, "and now Mother is in a memory impairment unit. I visit her every day, but she doesn't know who I am. I feel like she is a ship sailing into unknown waters, just a speck on the horizon, while I am stranded on the shore. If they don't find a cure for this disease, I hope I die before I get it."

One day a couple who live in my retirement community stopped in the hall to tell me about the strain that caring for his aged aunt has caused them. "We thought all our worries were over when we came here to retire," Martha said, "but caring for her has caused us so much stress." Paul remarked, "It seems as if we are going and coming every day, victims of her constant complaints." They both looked old and tired beyond their years.

In 2008 the Alzheimer's Association estimated that as many as 5.2 million people in the United States were living with Alzheimer's disease. In 2007 nearly 10 million women and men provided 8.4 billion hours of unpaid care at home for loved ones suffering from Alzheimer's or other dementia. Seventy percent of people with Alzheimer's live at home, cared for by family members and friends. Experts predict that by 2010, almost half a million cases will be diagnosed each year, and one of eight baby boomers will develop this disease. If you haven't yet been a caregiver, you likely will be one.

The number of people caring for loved ones with dementia will skyrocket in the next few years because people are living longer, and the baby boom generation is aging. The odds of developing a dementing disease *double every five years* beyond age sixty-five, although dementia may occur much earlier. Alzheimer's disease is now the sixth leading cause of death in the United States, and the fifth leading cause of death for people over sixty-five. Nearly 50 percent of the population will develop a dementing disorder by age eighty-five. Geriatricians predict that if a cure is not found by 2050, as many as *sixteen million* Americans will have some form of dementia, with Alzheimer's being the most prevalent.

The number of people caring for loved ones with dementia will skyrocket in the next few years because people are living longer, and the baby boom generation is aging.

For a long time, brain disease was a taboo subject. Families who dealt with dementia kept it within the family circle or told others that "Mother has some memory problems and gets confused," or "Dad has hardening of the arteries."

Regardless of whether they are cared for at home or in a memory care facility, persons with dementia become aliens to society, trapped in their own world, like the lepers of Jesus' time. For these persons, it is literally "out of sight, out of mind" or "out of their minds, out of our sight." Until recently, institutional care was based on a custodial mode.

A great deal of time and money has been spent to secure adequate physical care for people with a dementing illness. This has resulted in treating the *biol-*

ogy of their disease, rather than focusing on the needs of individuals and their families. As Peter J. Whitehouse has so well stated, "To bring about a new framework that can help us adapt to aging in the twenty-first century, Alzheimer's disease has to be talked about, brought out into the open, and seen from a more enlightened perspective."[1] Such a perspective includes nourishing the spirits of those afflicted with this disease, and offering ways to have a meaningful relationship with loved ones who can no longer remember us.

Though dementia affects the mind and the body, it cannot destroy the soul. Unfortunately, our society treats persons with dementia as if they have no souls. Nothing is further from the truth. Their brains may be wasting away, but their souls are still alive. So where can persons recently diagnosed with dementia find help when they ask, "What will happen to my faith when I can no longer remember?" How do we respond to caregivers who ask, "Why has God let this happen to us?" or "How can I go on believing in the goodness of God when I see my mom (dad) suffering from a disease that destroys their memory and the person I know?" Our responses demand spiritual, not medical or scientific, answers.

Persons with dementia and caregivers need to find a source of living water lest their spirits die, parched from the ravages of the mind or from the draining burden of caregiving. In a real sense, both care receivers and caregivers are on a mutual path. We could compare them to the Samaritan woman who came to the well of Sychar in the midday heat (John 4:4-42). She went there alone at a time she thought no one else would be present. Similarly, persons with dementia are forced into noon-time loneliness by their exclusion from the rest of society. Caregivers often face their struggles alone, with little or no help from others, sometimes not even from family members.

The Gospel of John records that the Samaritan woman met a stranger (Jesus) at the well. He surprised her by asking her for a drink. (We tend to forget that persons with dementia can offer us spiritual gifts from the depths of their souls, which remain intact.) Jesus turned the conversation toward the gift of living water, which he alone could give. Only this "living water" could satisfy the deep thirst of her soul and give strength for her hard life. Like the woman at the well, caregivers desperately need living water—spiritual help—so they can continue offering care to those they love.

Caregivers are fellow travelers with their loved ones into this unknown land that the psalmist called the "land of forgetfulness" (Ps. 88:12). Only God, who became incarnate in Jesus of Nazareth, can give us the kind of spiritual support we need, and as we become Christ to our loved ones, "the least of these," we provide the same kind of spiritual care.

My Experience: Richard

My involvement with dementia began in the 1960s when I was a distant caregiver for my mother, who suffered from Parkinson's dementia. Her shaking hands, expressionless face, and ability to speak only a few words still haunt me. I can identify with the struggles of distant caregivers, who must deal with a myriad of feelings when they cannot be present with their loved one. I felt guilty because my father and sister, a psychiatric nurse, bore all the burden. All I could offer were sporadic visits, calls, and letters until my mother no longer knew who I was. As she drifted into her own world of shadows, I asked how a loving God could allow this beautiful woman, who had spent her life serving her family, to suffer so. When we had to put her in a nursing home, I prayed that God would send angels to take her to heaven. She died in her sixty-sixth year, and my prayer was answered.

I did an internship as a chaplain's assistant in what was then called a sanatorium. I visited the "patients" and tried to listen to their garbled language. Some of them thought I was their son. One woman insisted that Harry Truman, a former president of the United States, was her brother. She kept asking me to write him and tell him to get his sister out of this place. I refused to do so. (In retrospect, I wish I had gone along with her request and said, "Tell me what it was like to be Truman's sister when you were children," or, "How often did you visit your brother in the White House?" thus entering her world and forgetting mine.) One of my assignments was to hand out hymnals to the residents and then to collect them as they left worship. The same woman slammed the hymnal into my hands and said angrily, "Here, chaplain, take this hymnbook and cram it!" At that time, little was known about dementia.

Yet I imagine most of the patients there suffered from this disease of the brain.

Later I served as a chaplain in a nursing home and then as a volunteer in two other care facilities. I learned much from those experiences. Once as I attempted a homily during a worship service, a woman in a wheelchair blurted out, "This is the nearest to nothing I ever heard in my life," and promptly wheeled out of the chapel, followed by most of the residents. That soon ended my homilies for people with dementia.

As I continued a ministry there and to other nursing homes, I began to have an uneasy feeling that any communication with these people never got through to them. I remember a lady the staff called "Mrs. Paper Face" who roamed the halls, never spoke, and had a blank stare on her face. She was typical of most people in the nursing homes.

Around that time, my wife, Alice Ann, became the primary caregiver for her mother, who had dementia and was placed in a care facility. I wondered how Alice Ann would manage to balance the unending demands of her mother plus those of our family, and teach at a middle school. Her two brothers offered little help. That was when I had a firsthand experience of the primary caregiver, who somehow had to juggle all those demands and make it through the days and nights. All I could do was support my wife and offer a sense of humor and my presence.

Now Alice Ann and I live in a continuing care retirement community where forty residents with Alzheimer's disease and related dementias live in comparative isolation from other residents. I feel God's call to be their advocate and caregiver, and this calling has become a "vocation within a vocation" and my passion for my later years. I sense a loving acceptance and common feeling among these dear people that deeply touches me. Yet it saddens me to see them look in the mirror but see no one there, and those haunting eyes that say, "Talk with me; I'm still in here."

My greatest learning has not come from textbooks or classes but from the residents themselves. They will never know my name, but they know my presence, and I see love in their eyes when I say their names and listen to them. I believe that people with dementia mirror our own lives—we sometimes feel bewildered and lost, forgetful, and incoherent. And, like these often neglected persons, we need to give and receive love.

Last year Kim Kelly, campus director, and I initiated an Alzheimer's support group at Redstone Highlands, the retirement community where I live. Sponsored by the Alzheimer's Association, our group meets once a month. Every month some of the caregivers return, and others begin attending. I have listened to their heart-wrenching stories of the burden they bear for their loved ones who suffer with this disease. I have preached or led seminars in many churches and community agencies. Caregivers tell me that they have found legal and medical assistance for their issues, but nowhere can they find emotional and spiritual support.

My Experience: Jane

I can't remember a time when older adults didn't influence my life. My parents were older than most new parents in 1946—my mother was thirty-seven; my father, forty-eight. I was their first and only child. They were the youngest children in their own families; there was a twenty-year spread between my parents and their oldest siblings! As a result, my aunts and uncles were old enough to be my grandparents, and my youngest cousin was fifty when I was born. My mother often jokingly told me that I was sixty when I was born, referring to a kind of old-fashioned thinking and attitude I developed because my "playmates"—until I entered school—were older adults. Neither of my parents lived to age sixty-five; both of them had died by the time I was sixteen. By that time, most of my relatives had also died. A few suffered strokes, and one cousin died at age forty-six of early-onset Alzheimer's disease, but I did not know about her dementia.

My first personal encounter with dementia occurred in the mid-1970s when I was hired as a case manager for a senior services agency in Boston. I reported to work on the first day, eager to help older adults by providing enough in-home services to keep them out of nursing homes. I visited my first clients, a seventy-five-year-old woman and her ninety-six-year-old mother, in their home. The women were friendly, inviting me into their antique-filled living room and even offering tea. I spent an hour and a half with them, assessing their home-care needs, and felt quite satisfied with myself as I took the subway back to the office. I did notice that they continually contradicted each other and repeatedly asked me the same questions, but I attributed this to the cognitive decline of aging, which I thought was normal.

When I returned to the office, the agency director was standing at my desk waiting for me. "What happened?" he asked with a worried expression and a concerned voice. "Oh, it went fine," I replied. "They are really nice ladies, and I think we can provide them with what they need to stay at home."

"No, that's not what I mean," he said. "A few minutes ago I received a telephone call from the daughter saying that you had stolen $5,000 from them. She said there was a paper bag with cash in it on the couch where you sat, and after you left, it was gone. They believe you stole their money!"

I was shocked. I couldn't imagine why these clients had "turned" on me, and I was in a predicament, for it was their word against mine. They decided to sue the agency. Fortunately, the director insisted on having their cognitive abilities assessed. They were diagnosed with an early form of dementia, and to my relief the lawsuit was dropped. I was tempted to quit and forget about working with older adults, but I needed the job.

Fortunately, that was my only really negative experience. Over time, I encountered many older adults who were grace-filled examples of aging, and I became optimistic about my own future elderhood.

My first experience left a lasting impression; it sparked a growing interest in the psychology of older adults. I decided to enter the relatively new field of aging and earned master's degrees in counseling psychology and gerontological social work and a PhD in clinical gerontology. After completing my doctorate, I took a position as a faculty member and clinical gerontologist in the Department of Family and Geriatric Medicine at the University of Louisville School of Medicine and as an adjunct faculty member in the School of Social Work. For nearly thirty years I have taught behavioral and social gerontology, conducted research, and provided clinical services such as psychosocial evaluation and counseling to older adults and their families. I have spent a good deal of time working with caregivers of people with dementing diseases.

In 1984 I helped develop and now direct our Geriatric Evaluation and Treatment Program, which enables older adults to have an in-depth evaluation of memory, physical, and emotional status, and environmental safety, as well as an assessment of caregiver burden and resources. In this multidisciplinary program, which uses a team approach to evaluation, one of my responsibilities has been to test the cognitive and emotional functioning of our older patients, most of whom suffer from some form of dementing disease. After the testing, I explain the results, offer memory rehabilitation exercises, suggest appropriate community resources, and counsel each person about the disorder and its implications for patient and family.

I serve on the Kentucky Institute on Aging and the Kentucky Alzheimer's Disease Council; I also teach a

"Pastoral Responses to Aging" course at Louisville Presbyterian Theological Seminary as needed. On a more personal note, for twenty years both my husband and I were caregivers of my mother-in-law, who suffered from stroke-related dementia in the last years of her life, until her death in 2003.

My passion, however, is the spiritual domain—the possibility of spiritual growth and development in the later years—and I love to give retreats and workshops on this subject. Desiring to offer more individualized spiritual care, I received training to become a spiritual director for older adults and their caregivers. All of this work is my vocation, my calling, and now that my sixties have arrived and I'm in the "aging baby boomer" category, I have an even more personal reason for dedicating myself to this calling. Throughout this book I will share what I have learned about life and about God from persons with dementia and from their caregivers.

Social and Spiritual Significance of This Book

Richard and I think this book holds special significance for the ultimate well-being of older adults (present and future) who have been diagnosed with dementia, and for their professional and family caregivers. We both frequently hear some variation of the following comment, said with an attempt at humor but truly intended: "I've told my kids that if I ever get into this situation (dementia), I want them to take me behind the barn and shoot me." Others state outright that they are already stockpiling medications to end their lives if they are diagnosed with any dementing disease. We fear that these threats are real—that as the baby boomers age and develop cognitive losses, they truly will take their lives in their own hands and end them.

We also firmly believe that the last lesson parents teach their children is how to die well—and gracefully. We have known parents who ended their lives, ostensibly for the benefit of their families. These suicidal deaths almost always traumatize those left behind, even if they agree with the "rationality" of the suicide. No suicide can compare with a good hospice or pastorally accompanied death. We hope this book will provide elders and their caregivers with a different, more hopeful model of dealing with life and death in the realm of dementia.

1

GIVING AND RECEIVING CARE

Six days before the Passover Jesus came to Bethany, the home of Lazarus, whom he had raised from the dead. There they gave a dinner for him. Martha served, and Lazarus was one of those at the table with him. Mary took a pound of costly perfume made of pure nard, anointed Jesus' feet, and wiped them with her hair. The house was filled with the fragrance of the perfume. But Judas Iscariot, one of his disciples (the one who was about to betray him), said, "Why was this perfume not sold for three hundred denarii and the money given to the poor?" . . . Jesus said, "Leave her alone. She bought it so that she might keep it for the day of my burial. You always have the poor with you, but you do not always have me."

—John 12:1-8

T his is *not* the way it was supposed to be!" blurted an anguished middle-aged woman, half to herself and half to me (Jane), as we stood at the clinic elevators. I recognized her as Marian, the daughter of a member of our congregation who had recently been diagnosed with Alzheimer's disease. She appeared harried, frustrated, totally at her wits' end. "Not the way you expected?" I responded.

"No! I was supposed to enjoy my retirement. But I'm spending all my time taking my mother to her medical appointments. I'm here today to pick up a prescription for a new memory pill. There's just no time for me; I feel trapped, and I'm burning out fast. My own doctor told me that caregivers often die before the person they're caring for. Is that what I have to look forward to?"

Marian was so stressed that I too was worried about her health and well-being. "Let's go down to the snack bar for some coffee," I suggested. "Maybe we can figure out something that will help." Marian hesitated. "I left Mom with a sitter she doesn't like, but I guess she'll be all right for a little while longer. I really do need to talk with someone, and I need some caffeine too!"

As we sat together in the snack bar, Marian described the frustration, hopelessness, and helplessness she felt in her role as the fifty-six-year-old caregiver of an eighty-five-year-old mother with dementia. "How far along is she?" I asked, suddenly realizing that this is the same question we often ask about pregnant women.

"About the beginning of the second stage, her doctor thinks. She still knows where she is and has very lucid moments, but she absolutely refuses to leave her home for a place where she can get the care I can't give her. Now it's becoming dangerous for her to live alone, but she won't have anyone live with her either. I'm afraid her doctor is going to report me to Adult Protective Services for neglecting to provide twenty-four-hour care for her. I'm an only child, so I've had to take early retirement to care for her. I feel like I'm neglecting my own family. Because of her dementia, she has absolutely no idea how much caring for her is costing me—emotionally, physically, socially, and spiritually, let alone financially—to keep up the pretense that she is 'independent,' nor does she even seem to care!

"It wouldn't be so bad if she could get better, but she just gets worse! She's really not the mother I've always known; it's as though a demanding stranger has invaded her body. Caring for her seems like such a waste of time and effort—I wish she would just die. We treat our animals better than we do old people; at least it's legal to put them out of their misery."

Then Marian wailed, "I feel so guilty admitting all of this to you—she is my mother, after all! But really, what's the use of living so long when you can't enjoy it? Why must I waste years caring for someone who eventually won't even know me? I've told my own kids that if I ever get like her, they need to take me behind the barn and shoot me! I never want to burden my kids this way." She paused to take a breath and continued. "I hope I'm not shocking you, but I feel like I'm at the end of my rope. I haven't had anyone to talk to, no one who has any inkling of what my life is like now!"

I wasn't shocked. Marian's story and others like it are increasing and will continue to do so as our population ages. The cries of anguished caregivers begging for help of all kinds, especially for some glimpse of meaning in their devotion to loved ones who have lost memory and independent functioning, are all around. Sometimes they are silent cries into pillows in the middle of the night. All caregivers have two basic needs: (1) affirmation that their caregiving is not in vain, and (2) reassurance that the lives of those they care for are not being lived in vain.

As an aging specialist working with older adults and their caregivers, as well as a caregiver of my own mother-in-law, I felt overwhelmed by Marian's suffering. I knew only too well all the negative feelings and concerns that Marian shared. But I also had the benefit of thirty years of watching the caregiving and receiving process "play out." I had the benefit of having participated in the care of my mother-in-law, and I knew that something deeply positive, renewing, and meaningful could come out of what appears to be a no-win situation.

The only help I could offer Marian that afternoon was my presence and my listening ears. She did not need advice or referral to a social service agency, nor did she want to hear my own story. She was desperate for someone to pay complete attention to her and listen to what she was going through, for as long as she needed to talk. "You and all my mother's friends from church must think I am coldhearted for not taking her into my own home, but we have no room! I am glad that at least one of you knows the other side of the story. Thanks for listening; I don't feel quite as tempted to run away, and now I can get this prescription filled."

I sat for a while, reflecting on the plight of caregivers and care receivers when a dementing disorder has invaded their lives. Another source of caregiver anguish came to mind—that of the person who has had to place a loved one into a nursing home and finds it increasingly difficult to force themselves to visit. "I just don't go anymore," Harold had told me during a counseling session. "Mother doesn't even know who I am, and it really tears me up emotionally. When she remembers her car but not me, I'm a total basket case after I visit her. Why should I bother putting myself through that when it's just a waste of my time? She gets good care and thinks the aides are her mothers. I don't have to be there; it wouldn't make any difference if I never showed up again!" Then he broke down, crying, "I miss my mother!"

Still another caregiver, one of my spiritual directees, had wailed, "I am furious with God for letting this happen to my husband! He's been such a good man, devoted to our church. God is just not present in this situation—and neither are those church members my husband served."

How do we respond to such cries of broken hearts and tired lives? Can we offer any answer, any consolation, any words to sustain the caregivers of parents, spouses, relatives, and friends so that their once-strong bonds of mutual relationships can somehow survive? How can we come to see this disease—a tsunami that ultimately wipes away all self-knowledge—through the eyes of God?

In response to these questions, the first thing I want to say is that *God does not cause anyone to suffer from dementia* (or any other disease, for that matter). Illness is part of our human condition, and God has given us brains to put to use in eradicating this disease. Someday we will know what causes Alzheimer's and other dementing diseases and have effective treatments for them. A cure will be found. The current generation just happens to be caught in the "pre-cure" time. Now our task is to deal with the situation—individually and as a community—as best we can, just as we did with pneumonia and other infectious diseases before the discovery of antibiotics.

How can we come to see this disease— a tsunami that ultimately wipes away all self-knowledge— through the eyes of God?

Second, dementia is probably one of the most spiritually and theologically challenging of all illnesses because it calls into question the nature of personhood. It causes us to ask such questions as: "Who am I when I can't name things and don't know what they are? Who am I when I can't think, can't love, and can't even respond to love? Who am I when I don't know who I am?"

A secular person's response to these questions might be: "You are no one. Your body is intact, but the person you once were is gone. You are a walking shell, of little worth to yourself, to your loved ones, to the whole community." In this way of thinking, the soul—identified with the rational mind—has vanished. Such thinking leads to the ultimate question, "Why should we bother caring for a body devoid of a self, of humanity, of a soul?"

But is the rational, thinking mind—consciousness—really the soul, or even the self? Early Greek thinkers (if they were still around) might say, "Yes!" and might have no trouble discarding the leftover (still living) body. They thought dualistically, where things were black and white, yes or no, alive or dead.

In Judeo-Christian thinking, however, the body and soul are united until death. After death, we are not complete until we are in our resurrected bodies! (Yes, we are promised bodies after our own resurrection—a sometimes forgotten promise!) What does this way of thinking tell us about dementia, the person with dementia, and the caregiver? It means that the body, which may require total care for all functions, continues to be united with the soul. The person in the last stages of dementia is not an empty shell. God's child continues to exist, even though in a state yet unknown to those who love him. Even if we can't "contact" the person to interact with him, God continues to hold this beloved child in the palm of God's hands. At some level the person lives deeply in the mystery of God, in intimate connection with God's love, without the distractions of the world around him.

In a previous book, *10 Gospel Promises for Later Life,* I wrote about a friend who is a nursing assistant in a dementia care unit. A patient she was helping to dress asked her, "Honey, what's my name?" My friend told her, and the woman replied cheerfully, "Oh, that's right! Half the time I don't even know who I am." Then she pointed to a cross on her wall and affirmed emphatically, "But he does, and that's all that counts!" At that moment the woman with dementia was a pure witness to the love of God for all of us. As we care for people with dementia, whether they be family, friends, or patients, we need to keep in mind that even though they may not know who they are or who we are, God knows—and that is what matters most.

Caring for those with dementia presents a major challenge to our own faith. It tests whether we can trust that God will take care of us if we are ever in the same situation. It tests whether we can love unselfishly, without asking for any love back for ourselves. It also tests whether we can love lavishly without expecting anything in return, without paying attention to the cost, knowing that no act of love is ever wasted. Any loving action puts love into the world. The deed doesn't need to be acknowledged in order to be effective. We don't need to be recognized as the lover. We don't need to be thanked for our love to be helpful. We love, not for our own satisfaction but for the pure act of pouring out love lavishly on the object of our love. If our love doesn't have visible results, that doesn't matter. Love has gone out into the universe. Ultimately, the act of loving will affect us, because loving, without any expectation of return, changes us, stretches us, transforms us. It teaches us to love as Christ loves.

In the final analysis, the experience of loving a person with dementia is a unique, mutual spiritual path. It is a spiritual path in which we learn to love generously, without constraint, without praise or thanks, sometimes despite a slap in the face. It leads us to our own freedom. Reaching this point spiritually is not easy. It requires self-care; it does not ask for martyrdom. It may require our relinquishment of "ownership" of our loved one enough to let others help with their care. It may also require us to say no to a person's demands when they are not in his or her best interest or when what the person asks is beyond our physical, mental, or financial capacity to provide. This is when love becomes "tough love."

In the final analysis, the experience of loving a person with dementia is a unique, mutual spiritual path.

The best example of such lavish love is the Gospel story of Mary of Bethany, who breaks her expensive alabaster jar of perfume and rubs it all over Jesus' feet. The disciples become furious at such "waste," saying that the money she spent on the perfume could have been used to feed the poor (something practical, useful). How does Jesus respond? He gratefully and graciously accepts Mary's sacrifice, knowing the love with which she has given it. She poured her own costly love into the world, and that's what mattered to Jesus. Those of us who care for persons with dementia can do the same, with this woman as our patron saint.

Reflection

1. Have you ever felt like Marian—expecting one kind of retirement and finding another?

2. How have your caregiving responsibilities affected your faith?

3. When have you felt that your caregiving was an act of futility?

4. What meaning have you made of your caregiving experience?

5. How does the assertion that "no act of love is ever wasted" enable you to look at caregiving differently?

2

FACTS AND FALLACIES
ABOUT DEMENTIA

Jesus took the blind man by the hand and led him out of the village; and when he had put saliva on his eyes and laid his hands on him, he asked him, "Can you see anything?" And the man looked up and said, "I can see people, but they look like trees, walking." Then Jesus laid his hands on his eyes again; and he looked intently and his sight was restored, and he saw everything clearly.

—Mark 8:23-25

Jesus healed the blind man of Bethsaida in stages. At first he healed him of blindness, but the man could not see things clearly, since people looked like trees walking. His vision was obscured, and objects at a distance looked blurry. Ophthalmologists call this condition myopia—having good nearsighted vision but poor distance vision. As one who has had two cataract surgeries, I (Richard) am quite familiar with clouded lenses that have lost their elasticity and made distant objects appear fuzzy. It took a second touch from Jesus for the man to see people and trees, not people who looked like trees walking.

Although the man's healing was physical, it had spiritual meaning for Jesus' disciples. They still did not really understand who Jesus was. Even when Peter confessed Jesus as the Messiah, he had no concept of a suffering Messiah. Jesus might have said to the disciples, "You know, this blind man is just like you!" They became cleared-sighted after the Resurrection when they received the spiritual insight to know Christ's true identity. The healing of their minds and hearts was a gradual process.

The same is true of dementia. Many fallacies about this brain disease prevail among some professional and family caregivers. We need a second touch, a spiritual insight, to realize the value of these persons that our society so often misunderstands, stigmatizes, and labels. For example, we often call them "dementia patients" instead of "persons with dementia."

This reminds me (Richard) of the Jewish philosopher Martin Buber's contrast of how human beings relate to others. According to Buber, we relate to others either as "I-It" or "I-Thou." If we relate to people as I-It, we see them as subjects, which causes detachment and separateness. This becomes a way of relating to people with dementia, if we see them only as objects to be treated. If we treat them as I-Thou, we do not see them in this way but as subject-to-subject, persons who need love.

At times, society and medical professionals objectify persons with dementia and see only this disease. They do not realize that, regardless of the stage of dementia, these are still persons with souls who often have a spirituality we do not possess. We may yearn for a deeper spirituality but fear expressing ourselves in ways that move beyond our intellect.

In this chapter we seek to separate fact from fallacy about dementia so that all who care for persons with dementing diseases will be able to see them as persons, not merely as objects to be treated. We will give a brief overview of dementia and answer some of the most frequently asked questions we hear from caregivers.

Question 1: Will everyone eventually get dementia if they live long enough?

My (Jane's) qualified answer is no—advanced age does not automatically sentence one to living in a state of unknowing. That said, current research does show that about 47 percent of persons who live to age eighty-five and beyond develop a dementing disease. Unfortunately some people, including physicians, continue to believe the fallacy that everyone will lose their memory if they live long enough. We still hear patients bemoan that their doctors fail to take seriously their complaints of memory loss, dismissing their fears with remarks like, "What do you expect? You're eighty-five!"—as though loss of memory that interferes with one's daily life is a normal aspect of the aging process about which nothing can be done. Not necessarily so! Let's look at three basic and important facts about aging and mental ability.

- *Fact 1.* Cognitive changes (the ability to think, remember, and problem-solve) are age-related. Positive and negative changes occur throughout life. Negative changes in cognition do not necessarily mean a person suffers from dementia.

- *Fact 2. Dementia* is a general word used to describe a variety of progressively damaging brain diseases, which share some, but not all, characteristics.

- *Fact 3.* Even though research shows that about 47 percent of all persons who live to be eighty-five and older will develop a dementing disease, there are measures one can take to delay, lessen the severity, and perhaps even prevent its occurrence.

Take a closer look at Fact 1—the relationships between cognitive changes and aging. Some are obvious. For example, it is easier for a four-year-old to learn a second language than it is a twenty-year-old. A teenager's video game and text-messaging prowess reaches its peak by age twenty-five. Yet, a male teen's abilities to problem-solve and to think and plan ahead does not mature until the mid-twenties. Speed of recall (as in the ability to remember the name of the person walking toward you at your twenty-fifth high school reunion) begins to decline as early as the forties. Difficulty distinguishing between two different stimuli (such as trying to converse with someone while in a noisy restaurant) is common in the fifties and sixties, as is the ability to retrieve words quickly on demand. In the seventies, eighties, nineties, and beyond, the short-term memory (for example, remembering where you parked your car in a large parking lot) often suffers. It takes longer to retrieve both short- and long-term memories. And, while you are still perfectly able to learn new material that interests you, it takes longer to categorize new information, store it, memorize it, and retrieve it. You may also have problems with organization and planning in daily life.

Interestingly, there are gender differences in the types of cognitive changes. Men may experience a decline in their ability to problem-solve, while women notice a lessening of their ability to process information quickly. One major positive difference between young and old is that while the young may have excellent short-term memory, they may not recognize patterns of recurring events. Elders, who have had many years of storing the generalities and idiosyncrasies of events, may have trouble with short-term recall but remember patterns more effectively. This may be the physiological basis for the wisdom that comes with age. For example, a physician right out of medical school may not recognize a rare disease she has merely read about and memorized from a textbook, but the sixty-year-old doctor who has seen the disease just once in his lifetime is likely to be able to recognize and diagnose it! The good news is that the negative changes seniors experience, as irritating and sometimes embarrassing as they may be, are not necessarily signs of early dementia.

Fact 2: There are many types of dementia. Dementia is a general term encompassing a variety of diseases with similar symptoms but different causes. The most common and well-known type of dementia is Alzheimer's disease (AD), which makes up from 50 to 70 percent of all cases of dementia. Other kinds include frontotemporal dementia (FTD), dementia with Lewy bodies (DLB), vascular dementia (VaD), mixed (AD and VaD), Creutzfeldt-Jakob disease (CJD), and the dementias that may accompany Parkinson's disease (PD), normal pressure hydrocephalus (NPH), Huntington's disease (HD), and Wernicke-Korsakoff Syndrome (WKS).

These diseases are similar in that they involve a progressive mental decline and share many of the following characteristics:

1. Mental and functional decline from a previously higher level;

2. Mental and functional decline severe enough to interfere with work, hobbies, social interaction, and other aspects of daily life;

3. Decline in more than one of the following four primary mental abilities:

   > Recent memory—ability to retain and recall new information;

   > Comprehension—ability to understand and/or use language via speaking, reading, or writing;

   > Visuospatial skills—ability to translate visual symbols into knowledge of place and time;

   > Executive function—ability to problem-solve, focus on a task, organize, plan, and reason.

The following may also occur:

4. Changes in personality;

5. Changes in mood or behavior;

6. Apathy or loss of initiative;

7. Problems with abstract thinking.

A commonly used term to describe early changes in mental status is *mild cognitive impairment* (MCI). This term refers to mild losses of the above mental abilities that are obvious to the person as well as to employers, friends, and/or family and can be measured by detailed evaluation. Many, but not all, sufferers of MCI continue to decline.

Fact 3: We can take preventive measures. There are things we can do to forestall, lessen, or even prevent the development of a dementing disorder, even if one or more of our relatives has dementia. First, the Alzheimer's Disease Association teaches that a heart-healthy lifestyle is also good for one's brain. This is especially true for vascular and mixed forms of dementia—keeping clear pathways to the brain is as essential to the brain's health as to the heart and the rest of the body. A combination of a heart-healthy diet, regular exercise, lowered cholesterol, and management of hypertension is essential for brain health. Recent research suggests that in addition to the above recommendations, thirty minutes of intensive cardiovascular exercise per day, combined with frequent social interaction, may forestall the development of AD. This is really good news, perhaps not for those already suffering from the diseases of dementia, but certainly for their caregivers and anyone who worries about developing dementia.

Question 2: Is medical care the greatest need of persons with dementia?

All human beings, no matter their age, have four common needs: (1) to protect and nurture the body, (2) to love and be loved, (3) to have a place or role in society, and (4) to be connected to God, a Higher Power, or something beyond oneself. Medical care falls in category 1. There is no doubt that medical care—diagnosis, treatment, and palliative care—is essential for persons with dementia, but it is not what they need most.

Along with appropriate medical care is loving care, continued involvement with other people, and a sense of connection to a loving God. As the dementia progresses, needs change. For example, people in the early stages of any dementia are worried and often frightened. If they are aware of their cognitive changes, they feel tremendous loss, possible anger—all of the emotions that correspond with loss of any kind. They need to be reassured that they will continue to be loved, no matter what happens. In addition, they need to be involved in all the decisions that must be made about their lives and their care. Are their wills—property and living wills—in order? How do they want to spend their days? What meaning can they make of this drastic change in lifestyle? They need, most of all, to be treated as normally as possible.

People in the middle stages, in which the disease has progressed to the point that people forget who they and their caregivers are, need to be kept safe and free of emotional anxiety. A constant, predictable environment should be provided. Mental and social stimulation must be continued. Pleasures should be maintained. People in the last stage, and those actively dying, need to be emotionally and physically comforted—kept company, kept warm, and kept free from pain and stress.

Question 3: Is there any way to communicate and continue a meaningful relationship with people who have dementia?

Absolutely. Communication is always possible, though the form it takes may change. One of the things that saddens me (Jane) most is to hear a caregiver say, "I no longer go to visit my mother (husband, wife, father, friend, etc.) because she (he) doesn't know who I am, doesn't understand what I say, can't talk. It's just a waste of time. I'd rather remember her as she was before she got this disease!" This may be true for objective communication, which becomes increasingly difficult as the dementing disease progresses. However, there are other forms of communication that are deeper and even more real than the exchange of facts!

Strangely, some of my best memories of my mother-in-law are the daily visits I made to her while she spent her last six months of life in a nursing home, suffering from vascular dementia. Frankie's dementia was so severe that she didn't recognize any of us, including her three sons and many grandchildren. Confined to a wheelchair, she was refusing food, as she had forgotten what to do with it when it was in her mouth. Initially, the practical purpose of my visits was to keep an eye on the quality of her care in the facility, which was on my route to and from work. I took a very task-oriented approach to the visits and didn't expect much in terms of interaction. By the time I visited her at the end of each day, I was usually very tired and dreaded having to do one more task. I would go to the nurses' desk and inquire about her status, then go to her room for a "quick" visit. Usually she was sitting in her wheelchair, sometimes agitated, other times staring out into whatever space she could still see, as she had been partially blinded by a stroke.

There was not much to do, nor was there any conversation to be had, since Frankie was also deaf, so I began the habit of brushing her hair. (This was a familiar task—for years she had loved my fussing with her hair between visits to the beauty parlor.) As soon as I took her hands in mine and touched her shoulder to let her know I was with her, she responded by clutching my hand. Then I would stroke her thin hair and gently begin to brush it. Gradually she relaxed into the brushing, became calm, and began talking. Usually she talked about her parents and nine brothers and sisters, reliving scenes from her childhood. Interestingly, this daily hair-brushing ritual had a positive effect on me as well. It seemed that as I brushed her hair, I also symbolically brushed away the cares and stresses of my own day. Because there was nothing else to do, I was forced to live in the present moment with Frankie, and the experience was surprisingly relaxing.

By the time I finished, said good-bye, and returned to my car, I felt renewed. The hour spent with Frankie had been therapeutic for both of us, and neither of us had spoken a word. We had related on a much deeper level where words became irrelevant. She did not need to know who I was; she felt the love I extended to her through the hair brushing, and I received the rest and stress relief I needed. Something mysterious had happened to both of us, and it was very good. After a few experiences of this kind of interpersonal encounter, I began looking forward to our times together. They became oases of peace in my stressful days.

Was this a real relationship? I believe so. It wasn't the same kind of highly cognitive, fact-ridden, chatty, gossip-laced conversation on which we developed our earlier relationship, but it was just as real—and perhaps much more meaningful at a deeper level. This experience of mutuality reminds me of the Gospel scene in which Jesus washes the feet of the apostles. Jesus insists that Peter allow him to wash his feet and even says very strongly that if Peter does not allow Jesus to wash his feet, he cannot be Jesus' disciple! Somehow, when we allow ourselves to be cared for, the person doing the caring benefits in some way as well. Caregiving and care receiving are mutually beneficial! (We will discuss techniques of deeper, relational communication in a later chapter.)

Question 4: Have persons with dementia lost their souls?

No question is more important than this one, for it determines how family and professional caregivers relate to persons with dementia. Is there still a person remaining as the mind progresses through stages of dementia, or does dementia destroy the very qualities that make someone a person?

I (Richard) spoke with a distraught family member who felt that when her mother reached the later stages of Alzheimer's disease, she disappeared into a void. Sue told me, "This disease has not only taken her from her family, but it has robbed her of her own self. When she looks at herself in a mirror, she has no idea who the person is. It's as if Mother descended into a dark emptiness and got lost. Everything has left her—memory, speech, and mobility. She is just a shell, waiting to go to heaven. All I have left is a vague memory of who she was." It would have been inappropriate for me, as a listener, to disagree with what my friend said. Grief consumed her, as if her mother had already died, and all I could offer was a gentle touch, without saying a word.

Later, however, I consoled Sue by saying that although her mother's mental abilities had disappeared, I firmly believed that her soul was alive and well inside her frail body. Sue's mother still retained the fullness of her spirit, although this was not evident to the casual observer. Deprived of her mind, her frail body with her intact soul was like an old automobile parked with the engine running but without a driver. She was still a part of that vital person whose mind had been ravaged by dementia, and needed to be treated with dignity, as her transparent spirit was still "in there."

We live in a hypercognitive society characterized by excessive talking, mind work, and busyness. We are told to live in the moment and not dwell in the past. How can this maxim relate to people who have lost the present and do live in the past? So many people view persons with dementia as "out of mind, out of body." In other words, "out of their minds, and out of our sight." According to this philosophy, we should relegate persons with dementia to memory care facilities and treat them as bodies needing to be medicated, not as persons with spiritual needs.

I deeply believe that we must not let this disease of the brain define who people are. They are more than body and breath. They are living persons, born in the image of God, and they can be reached spiritually. At the end of life, their souls wait patiently for death, when the total person will be reunited with God and their lives unfold further in spirit. "For now we see in a mirror, dimly, but then we will see face to face. Now I know only in part; then I will know fully, even as I have been fully known" (1 Cor. 13:12).

Joni, who had lived a long time with dementia, made no response in our worship services, but when we blessed and touched her, saying, "The grace of God be with you," she smiled and said softly, "Thank you." We always felt her spirit hovered near to God and God's angels, and when she died, she slipped quietly "into that good night."[1] Now she is whole.

Question 5: Do traditional forms of worship relate to persons with dementia, and should these persons be offered the sacrament of Holy Communion?

If persons with dementia are perceived as persons with souls, then mainline churches have been negligent in their ministry to them. If we value these people as children of God, we must treat them as if they were still able to experience a relationship with God. We must believe that God will speak to even severely demented persons, if God so chooses.

Many persons with dementia who remain at home slip away from their faith communities and fall through the cracks. Family caregivers become embarrassed or uneasy when their loved ones with dementia act inappropriately during worship. They fear their loved ones will disrupt the service by saying something bizarre, so they leave them at home, where they languish without worship in a faith community.

Persons with early-stage dementia can still worship, even though the service gets more difficult for them to understand. They can often follow the order of worship, repeat the Lord's Prayer, sing hymns, and recite the Creed from memory. They can still be connected meaningfully to a faith community, and social contact is good for their brain health as well as self-esteem. Clearly, though, many members of faith communities know little about dementia and thus approach this disease with fear and avoidance.

A similar situation exists in long-term care facilities. Even when worship services are offered, they are either traditional forms of worship that do not touch the souls of persons with dementia, or kinds of worship that entertain but often demean. While it is true that some pastors, lay and ordained, do faithfully lead worship, the service is usually a conventional one that does not resonate with those whose mental powers have diminished. They may still hear the words, but their minds cannot grasp the meaning.

There is little doubt that music reaches beyond the dementia to a deeper place. The old hymns of the church, stored forever in the memory, remain. Music is usually the last thing to disappear. How often I (Richard) have witnessed persons in the last stages of dementia, ordinarily speechless, suddenly begin to sing the words of old, familiar hymns. I remember Nelda, an eighty-six-year-old woman who always seemed listless and unfocused. I nodded to her as she was placed in the front row, but she made no response. Midway through the service, we began to sing "Amazing Grace." Suddenly Nelda began to move her lips and then sing, articulating the words clearly, her voice strong. The caregivers were stunned; they had never heard her speak a word. Nelda's earlier experience in her childhood had connected with that hymn and been resurrected in the present moment. Since the association required no mental process, she could burst forth in song. It was as if the dementia that clouded her mind suddenly disappeared, and a ray of light shone through in the music.

Persons with dementia can resonate with other creative modes of worship. They may connect with the

Twenty-third Psalm, the Lord's Prayer, and other worship experiences from their childhood. Denied the ability to grasp words, persons with dementia often relate to symbols that remind them of the presence of God—the Bible, a cross or crucifix, icons, statues, flowers, sacred pictures, stained glass windows, candles, rosaries, and even the smell of incense—all speak to the senses of those who have cognitive impairment and cannot comprehend the meaning of words. (Creative modes of worship are further described in chapter 6.)

Denied the ability to grasp words, persons with dementia often relate to symbols that remind them of the presence of God.

The elements of the Lord's Supper, the bread and wine, (offered with caution, since some may choke), trigger religious memories of the past for people who belong to denominations that celebrate the Lord's Supper. However, we have encountered some clergy who do not offer the sacrament because they claim that persons with dementia do not understand what is happening. (Yet how many church members in their "right mind" really understand the sacrament?) Furthermore, the sacrament is a holy mystery, and who is to say that Christ cannot be present in the bread and wine to anyone who loves him? The sacrament of Communion is forever buried in their minds, and participation in this rite can be a deeply spiritual experience. Whenever I (Richard) offer the bread and wine, I speak the person's name and say, "This is my body broken for you." As I look into their eyes, I feel the presence of Jesus Christ.

When I lead worship for people with dementia, I always end with the old Sanskrit greeting *namaste* ("The God in me greets the God in you"). These children of God respond with the same words. True, their minds may not comprehend what *namaste* means, but God is present in their innermost being.

During worship services with people with dementia, I often recall that scene on Easter afternoon, when the disciples met behind locked doors for fear of the Romans and Jews. Bewildered by the events of the morning, they were almost out of their minds with disbelief and joy. Then Jesus suddenly appeared and said, "Peace be with you." As we pass the peace during the worship service, my mind returns to that moment in the upper room, for Christ is present even here beyond the locked doors, offering that same peace to these confused and bewildered minds.

Question 6: Do seminaries train clergy to minister to persons with dementia?

There is a simple answer to this question: no! In my experience (Richard's), few clergy of any church visit members with dementia. They may offer the sacrament of Communion and show up when members are dying or when death comes. But little consistent pastoral care is offered. Why do priests, ministers, and rabbis hesitate to spend time with their members who have dementia? No doubt clergy have problems accepting their own mortality, and persons whose minds have been ravaged make them aware of their own demise and the possibility that a similar fate awaits them if they visit people on the "other side."

Often clergy tell me they are too busy or unprepared to do pastoral care for their members with dementia, and they feel uncomfortable visiting members with dementia at home or in locked memory care facilities. One pastor remarked to me, "Why are you wasting your time with those people? They're out of it. They will never remember your name, and in ten minutes they will forget that you ever came to see them." But no act of love is ever wasted!

Sometimes little care is evident even around the time of death. Recently Jenny, the aunt of one of my (Jane's) friends, died after living in the dementia unit of a nursing home for five years. Until her illness she had been a faithful and active member of her congregation, a daily communicant of the Eucharist. She had been in the nursing home so long, however, that after a few years she was no longer considered a member of that congregation. Her beloved pastor retired, and when a new one was assigned to her church, no one told him that Jenny lived in a nursing home. After Jenny's death her family assumed that her funeral would take place at her church. But because she was no longer on the list of members, her family was told that her funeral could not be held at the church!

Perhaps the real burden of guilt should be laid at the door of theological education. Although churches of all faiths can expect to minister to an increasing number of members with dementia and to their families, little preparation is given in seminaries. Very few seminaries offer gerontology courses in their curriculum. A detailed survey of courses on pastoral care of older persons with dementia is beyond the scope of this book. Yet as the "graying of the church" reaches large proportions of members and their families in the next thirty years, theological education should make such courses a requirement, not an elective, for future pastors. Strategies for offering seminary courses on ministry to older adults are discussed further in chapter 7.

I (Richard) recall a young pastor telling me, "I'm going to visit all those old folks in the congregation and get that over with," as if it were a meaningless yet necessary task rather than an opportunity for pastoral care. As I spend time with persons with dementia, I ask myself this question: "If Jesus were here today, where would he be?" I am convinced that one of the places we would find Jesus is with persons with dementia.

An old legend in the Babylonian Talmud suggests an answer. Rabbi Joshua ben Levi came upon Elijah and asked him, "When will the Messiah come? . . . Where is he sitting?" Elijah replied, "He is sitting among the poor lepers." Where do we find Jesus today? We discover the answer in his words, "Truly I tell you, just as you did it to one of the least of these who are members of my family, you did it to me" (Matt. 25:40). We may well discover that caring for a person with dementia is a mutual spiritual path; they find Christ in us, and we in them.

Reflection

1. When have you been involved in an "I-It" relationship or encounter? Were you "I" or "It"? What did that feel like?

2. When have you been involved in an "I-Thou" relationship or encounter? Were you "I" or "Thou"? What did that feel like?

3. What fallacies or misconceptions did you have about dementia before reading this chapter?

4. What did you learn that had significance for your caregiving situation?

5. What questions do you still have about dementia? What resources are available to help you find answers to your questions?

3

CAREGIVING: A MUTUAL SPIRITUAL PATH

For the Caregiver

Then he poured water into a basin and began to wash the disciples' feet. . . . He came to Simon Peter, who said to him, "Lord, are you going to wash my feet?" Jesus answered, "You do not know now what I am doing, but later you will understand." Peter said to him, "You will never wash my feet." Jesus answered, "Unless I wash you, you have no share with me. . . . So if I, your Lord and Teacher, have washed your feet, you also ought to wash one another's feet."

—John 13:5-8, 14

For the Care Receiver

Jesus said to him], "Feed my sheep. Very truly, I tell you, when you were younger, you used to fasten your own belt and to go wherever you wished. But when you grow old, you will stretch out your hands, and someone else will fasten a belt around you and take you where you do not wish to go." (He said this to indicate the kind of death by which he would glorify God.) After this he said to him, "Follow me."

—John 21:17-19

The last chapter ended with the assertion that care-giving and care receiving can be a mutual spiritual path. How can this be? For guidance, I'll (Jane) examine the message Jesus was trying to get across to us in John 13—"Wash one another's feet!" Often this mandate of Jesus is interpreted to mean, "Wash your neighbor's feet. Wash as many feet as you possibly can. Wash everybody else's feet, but don't bother them with your own dirty feet. It is better to wash another's feet than to have your own feet washed." But is that what Jesus really told his friends to do?

In our power-hungry society, it feels better to give than to receive. When you're on the receiving end, you are in the power-less position.

The key words in this passage are "one another's feet," not just the other person's. When Peter refused to have his feet washed, Jesus told him that if he were not willing to be washed (if he were not willing to be cared for as well as to offer care), Peter could have nothing to do with him. Why was Jesus so adamant? Wasn't this a demonstration of humility on the part of Peter? Not really.

Think about how this biblical story relates to care-giving responsibilities. When you are doing something for another person, you have the power, the upper hand. You call the shots. And you get credit or status when other people observe your service. In our power-hungry society, it feels better to give than to receive. When you are on the receiving end, however, you are in the powerless position. Most people don't like to be in the receiving position because it makes them uncomfortable. But Jesus is telling us that to be his followers, we must at times give and at other times receive. How does this relate to the caregiving situation?

My Experiences of Foot Washing (Jane)

It may seem that the energy of caring (the foot washing) always goes out toward the person with dementia. But there are times when it comes back, and the caregiver is the recipient. The following story is an example of how my own feet were washed in a very powerful way.

A few years ago I was at a low point as a professional caregiver. I had been testing people with memory disorders and counseling them and their families for about fifteen years when I hit the proverbial wall. I was working too hard with very little play and felt burned out and jealous of others who seemed to be enjoying their lives so much more than I was. As a result I began to consider abandoning my work as a clinical gerontologist and opening a perfume shop! (I love perfume and reasoned that everyone who ventured into the shop would have a pleasant experience. No more telling people they have Alzheimer's. No more having to advise them to give up their driver's licenses. No more dealing with the pain and suffering of disconsolate caregivers!)

I prayed for God's guidance but did not receive a special calling to the perfume business. Instead, week after week I received nothing—no answer. Finally I begged God to let me know in some way what God really wanted me to do with my life. In that state of mind I pulled myself out of bed one morning and trudged back to another day of work. My first patient was a woman suffering from a form of dementia called primary progressive aphasia, thought to be a subset of Alzheimer's disease. This woman, who was accompanied by her daughter, had lost her ability to communicate both verbally and nonverbally. My task was to evaluate how much she understood of what she heard. As I went through the necessary tests, it became obvious that she was doing very poorly. Toward the end of the session I placed a pencil and paper in front of her and directed, "Please write a sentence for me." I knew she would not be able to do this, but the testing required that I at least go through the motions. She took the pencil and then looked at me. For what seemed like a very long and uncomfortable time, she just looked me in the eyes, as if studying me. She wrote nothing. Finally, just as I was about to retrieve the pencil and paper, she started to write. When she was finished, she slid the paper across the table to me and gave me a little smile, still looking intently at me. (I have to admit, it was a little unnerving.)

When I looked at what she had written, I could not believe my eyes. The sentence she had written was, "Enjoy your life—and help others too!" In addition, she had underlined every word. When I read the message, I gasped, "This is just what I needed to hear today; thank you so much!" Hearing my exclamation, her daughter grabbed the paper and said, "I needed that today too!"

We both took out our appointment books and wrote the sentence in them as reminders to care for ourselves as well as for others. A person suffering from the speechlessness of dementia helped me realize that I needed to have my feet washed too! When both her daughter and I told her that she had helped us that day, she seemed to feel affirmed, for she smiled for the rest of the session. This is an example of what Richard and I mean when we say that caregiving and receiving can be a mutual spiritual path.

My second incident of mutuality occurred with my mother-in-law, whose dementing disease was so advanced that she no longer recognized me or other members of her family. I wrote about how the simple act of brushing her hair calmed her and enabled me to be "in the present moment"—a very relaxing and renewing state. We both benefited from those visits. We washed each other's feet and were blessings to each other.

What I found is that most caregivers had stories to tell of spiritual gifts they had received from those for whom they were caring.

Neither of these shared moments was planned—by the grace of God they happened, and they surprised me. After these incidents, I began asking caregivers about their own experiences of being blessed by persons with dementia. What I found is that most caregivers—even those who were not particularly religious or spiritually oriented—had stories to tell of spiritual gifts they had received from those for whom they were caring. I was impressed by the excitement and joy with which they told their stories. I collect these stories as treasures to be savored and shared—they offer hope to me and to those with whom I share them. Because of my experiences and those shared with me, I have come to believe strongly that the soul of the person with dementia is no longer constrained or cluttered by her own ego needs. Even though her brain is damaged, she can become a pure, spontaneous, and unexpected conduit of God's love, an example of the Prayer of Saint Francis, which begins, "Lord, make me an instrument of thy peace."

Jesus' Promise

Jesus himself promised that we need not fear dependency and dementia in John 21:18, which was originally a proverb about aging. Interestingly, when this passage is read publicly, the last two lines are frequently omitted, leaving the hearer/reader with a dire (but all too often realistic) view of aging. Yet, these last two lines are wildly hopeful. Jesus tells Peter, to whom he is entrusting his mission ("Feed my sheep"), that one day he will be old and unable to care for himself (and will no longer be able to feed the sheep in the same active way). The passage paints a vivid picture of a person with dementia. You can almost see Peter, tied to his wife or daughter's apron strings so that he won't wander off in search of his beloved Jesus. To be told that someday he might not to be able to go where he wants to go to serve his Beloved must have been an agonizing prediction for Peter, who had just been given the keys of the kingdom and was ready to roll! Not to be able to serve—what kind of an end to a disciple's life is that?

But that is not the end of the story. Jesus assures Peter that even if he becomes old and someone else is in control of his life, he still will be able to glorify God! And he will glorify God specifically by means of this helpless state. What a fantastic yet mysterious promise! As Jesus promised Peter, the continued ability to glorify God is also promised to all lovers of God who suffer from a dementing disease—and to those who provide them with care. (We do know that Peter's fate was crucifixion, not dementia.)

Reenvisioning Caregiving/Receiving as a Mutual Spiritual Path

As I received increasing examples of the way persons with dementia witnessed God's love, I began to wonder, *Is there any way to reenvision caregiving, especially caring for a person with dementia, as an intentional spiritual path—an intentional mutual foot washing?* I realized that both the promise of the ill person's unceasing value to God and to God's purposes and Jesus' mandate to wash one another's feet are the building blocks of a mutual spirituality of caregiving and receiving.

Most discussion about caregiving focuses on the burdens of the caregiver and the negative effects on his or her health as a result of spending years in this role. Rarely is there mention of the positive aspects. I pondered these questions: *How can we deliberately make a paradigm shift from thinking of care for persons with dementia as a medical and social problem to viewing care as a spiritual opportunity, a challenge, an invitation for both caregiver and care receiver? How can we trust that caregiving is not an unwelcome glitch in a well-planned life? How can it be a way of living that is a mutual path of spiritual deepening, of coming closer to God, and of witnessing the love of God to each other and to the world? How can the person suffering from dementia participate?*

If you are seeking a deeper experience of God, looking for a way to make sense of dementia and what has become a seemingly senseless turn of events in your life, trying to find meaning in life, looking for a way to serve God, you are already on a spiritual path. However, you may not yet have envisioned your caregiving/receiving situation as an intentional, mutual spiritual path. How do you step out onto this mutual path? What do you have to do to claim this paradigm shift, this new way of looking at caregiving/receiving?

Four Basic Human Needs

Richard and I invite you to explore the idea of caregiving as a mutual spiritual path by first looking at the four basic human needs. As stated earlier, at every stage of life all persons have the following needs:

1. The physical need to protect and nurture the body;

2. The emotional need to give and receive love;

3. The social/intellectual need to have a place or role in society;

4. The spiritual need to be connected to God or to someone or something greater than themselves.

These four needs remain the same throughout the life span, but they are met in different ways at different stages of life. For instance, an infant's body needs to be protected and nurtured. He can't do it by himself, so his parents do it for him. Throughout adulthood, if he remains healthy, he takes care of his own physical needs. If he becomes sick at any age or frail in later life, this need may once again be another person's responsibility. The same is true for each of the other needs.

Similarly, in the caregiving situation, both the caregiver and the care receiver have the above needs. The care receiver needs to have her body cared for, protected, and nurtured. She needs to feel love. She needs to feel wanted or needed. She needs to know that God is on her side. The caregiver needs to care for, protect, and nurture her own body. She needs to love and receive love. She needs to have a role in society. She needs a relationship with God.

Often both the caregiver and receiver have helped meet each other's needs, especially if the receiver is a spouse. With dementia, the way these needs are met is often drastically disturbed. Sometimes the caregiver pays so much attention to the receiver that he neglects his own health. When his spouse doesn't recognize him as her husband, he may feel unloved. If he is no longer working or can no longer do volunteer work, he may feel roleless. He may also question God's caring and personal love as the disease progresses.

When you examine these basic needs in relation to your own life, ask yourself how well each of these needs is being met. Are there any gaping holes? Does the way the need is met need to be changed?

As examples, let's look at the way the need to love and be loved was transformed in the lives of two caregivers. Lucinda, a fifty-year-old wife and mother of three teen-aged boys, invited her mother to live with her. The two women had been best friends from the time of Lucinda's adulthood, and she was looking forward to continuing this closeness. However, because of the rapid progression of the mother's dementia, she no longer recognized Lucinda as her daughter and didn't even want her around. Lucinda was devastated and yearned in vain for her mother's love. Her husband and children loved her, but the special quality of her mother's love was gone. In the process of counseling her, I asked if she had a relation-ship with any other older woman. She told of an aunt—one her father's sisters—who had loved her as a child but whose company she had rarely sought because she had been so involved with her mother. I suggested that she attempt to resume the relationship. She did and found that while her aunt could never replace her mother's unique love, she was able to enjoy the older woman's company and received the gift of a new form of maternal love. And the experience of being loved by her aunt enabled Lucinda to love her mother more effectively.

James and his wife, Emily, had enjoyed fifty-five years of a good marriage when Emily was diagnosed with Alzheimer's disease. Since they had no children, James was her sole caregiver. As Emily's disease progressed and she needed more and more care, James found himself isolated from friends, church members, volunteer work, and even Emily, who no longer recognized him. He felt unloved and lonely. His pastor noticed James's isolation and the toll caregiving was taking on him, and he urged James to find a nursing home for Emily. Reluctant to do this for many months, James finally agreed to the move, which he thought would devastate both of them. What he found was something very different. When he allowed others to provide Emily with professional care, she began to interact more with her environment. She was no longer constantly irritated with James, and while she didn't recognize him as her husband, she talked with him and held his hand. They were able to have a different kind of loving relationship. In addition, James became friendly with the staff and joined the caregivers' support group sponsored by the home. There he found soul mates and developed friendships. His health and energy improved. After Emily's death he continued the friendships and worked as a volunteer at the nursing home twice a week. James found that he could not replace Emily's love, but he did find new ways to meet his need to give and receive love and to have a place in society.

These two stories demonstrate how our four basic needs are very fluid in the ways they can be met. It takes a little creativity (and often the help of others) to discover how to meet these needs anew when our usual ways are disturbed or destroyed.

Spiritual Needs

Let's focus now on the spiritual needs of caregivers and care receivers. First, I (Jane) need to tell you how I am defining and using the words *spiritual, spirituality, spiritual needs*, and *spiritual path*. There are a multitude of definitions of these popular, widely used, and rather vague words. The 1971 White House Conference on Aging asserted, "All [persons] are 'spiritual,' even if they have no use for religious institutions and practice no personal pieties." They defined the word *spiritual* as "pertaining to [one's] . . . ultimate concern, the basic value around which all other values are focused, the central philosophy of life . . . which guides a person's conduct, and the supernatural and non-material dimension of human nature."[1]

As with *spiritual*, there are many definitions of the term *spirituality*, and they often differ. In general, *spirituality* refers to a particular behavior, style, or attitude toward the sacred. It describes the way a person relates to God or that which is greater than self—transcendent reality. For my diverse-audience workshops I have created a working definition that is general enough to include people of most religions and philosophies—and those who do not subscribe to a religion. I start from a belief that all people have a physical body and a spirit, or soul or "true self," which is more than the body and lives after the death of the physical. My definition is this: "Spirituality is the way a person seeks, then either finds or creates, uses, and expands personal meaning in the context of the entire universe." In essence, spirituality is the way we answer and live out the perennial human question "Why am I here on earth?"

For the Christian, spirituality is the way a person responds to God's love. It is the process of seeking and enjoying a relationship with God the Creator (Father), God the Son (Jesus), and God the Holy Spirit (Spirit of Christ). It involves learning about God; opening to the experience of God's grace; loving and serving God, other people, and self; understanding and living life through the mind of Christ; and looking forward to being embraced by God in heaven throughout eternity.

The term *spiritual need* refers to the intensity of our yearning and/or searching for God and our response to God. It also alludes to anything we require to help us continue on our path toward a deeper relationship with the Divine.

Spiritual path also has many definitions. (Some people use the term *spiritual discipline*, but Richard and I prefer path.) The term can refer to any established pattern or institutionally approved route we adopt to engage in and develop our relationship with God. It can be as large as a life's vocation or as small as daily reading of scripture. (For example, the traditional callings of a missionary, a deacon, and a Sunday school teacher are three quite different, yet equally valid, spiritual paths.) Most spiritual paths prescribe specific disciplines or actions to enable us to (1) approach and respond to

God, (2) know our inner or true self, (3) find meaning, and/or (4) devote our life to the well-being of other individuals, society, and/or nature. Some of the more traditional personal spiritual disciplines include regular prayer, scripture reading, fasting, almsgiving, journal keeping, spiritual counsel, and so forth.

An Intentional Path

The caregiving/receiving situation in which we find ourselves when living with dementia is never a desired path, nor is it yet a well-recognized, intentional path to God recognized and supported by institutional religions. However, the fact that it (1) forces one to ponder the meaning of one's changed life, (2) brings together very intimately people who are committed to one another in some way, (3) often requires heroic acts of forgiveness and self-sacrificing love, (4) lasts for a long time, (5) involves a certain "dailiness" or patterned way of life, (6) always faces loss and death, and (7) is an ultimate response to Jesus' command to "love one another as I have loved you" makes it a perfect pathway to the experience of God's loving-kindness and nurturing care. As the number of older adults increases and as the baby boomers age and care for parents, spouses, and friends—and need care themselves—the idea that caregiving and receiving can be viewed as a mutual path to God rather than a negative interference in one's life can itself be life-giving.

When is it helpful to reenvision caregiving from burden to an intentional, mutual spiritual path? Anytime;

the earlier the better. But if you are actively trying to (1) find or create meaning in this drastic and unwanted change of your life plans, (2) understand how caregiving fits into your already established spiritual path, (3) understand how the very acts of caregiving can bring you closer to God, (4) nurture your beloved's spiritual needs, and/or (5) just plain survive physically, emotionally, and spiritually, now is the right time.

A Mutual Path

I (Jane) have shared stories of how persons with dementia can witness spontaneously to God's love, but can caregiving and receiving really be a mutual path? It is obvious that the caregiver can grow in relationship with God, but can the receiver, especially a person suffering from dementia, really grow spiritually? Richard and I believe so, especially in the early stages of the disease. Later, the caregiver becomes the presence of God and the provider of God's love to the person.

My friend Judy's Aunt Diana is a good example of spiritual growth in a person with early dementia. A childless widow, Aunt Diana had always dearly loved her sister's child, Judy, who was as emotionally close as any daughter could ever be. Even though Judy's home was ten hours away from Diana, who lived in a retirement community, they talked daily. Judy was Diana's power of attorney, health care surrogate, overseer of care, financial manager, recreation manager, buyer of clothes, and so forth. For eight years Judy had driven monthly to visit Aunt Diana and always stayed for the weekend. Aunt Diana looked forward to and enjoyed the visits and help, but she never seemed to realize just how much Judy, a busy executive, wife, civic leader, and grandmother, was sacrificing of her own life. And she never asked.

As her health declined, Aunt Diana grew increasingly dependent on Judy. Judy's visits became more frequent, due to health emergencies that required Diana's hospitalization. Each time Judy visited, Diana, who had been a lifelong, faithful, and active church member, would cry and wail, "I'm ninety-seven years old and good for nothing. Why doesn't God just take me home?" Finally Diana's physical and mental status declined so much that she needed to be relocated from assisted care to the nursing section of the facility. Judy needed help managing the move, so I volunteered, and we visited Aunt Diana the day of her transition to the nursing facility. The plan was that the following morning I would sit with Diana in her new room while Judy managed the removal of her aunt's furniture from her former apartment.

When we arrived, Aunt Diana was fretting about a drop-leaf dining table that had belonged to her great-grandmother. She wanted Judy to take it, but Judy didn't like the table, and she didn't have room for it in her home. She tried to convince her aunt to give it to another relative who had always admired it, but to no avail. Diana could not seem to understand why Judy would not take the table. Because Judy would not give in to her wishes, Diana pouted and became increasingly irritated with both of us. Finally we left, realizing that our presence was escalating her irritability, and wondering if it would have been kinder to Diana for Judy to lie about the disposition of the table! We both dreaded the following morning.

When we arrived at ten o'clock the next day, we found Diana still in bed, in nightclothes, with her hair a mess (she was usually a very neat lady who insisted on being dressed first thing in the morning). She was obviously in distress, and we thought it was due to the enormous change she had just experienced. When Judy asked her aunt what was wrong, Diana replied, "I've been talking and struggling with God all night long. I was so upset that you wouldn't take the table that I finally asked God what to do. I didn't like the answer he gave me, so we went back and forth all night about it. Early this morning I realized I was being selfish and unreasonable about the table. I knew you never liked it, but I wanted you to have it because it was your great-great-grandmother's. Shelly is kin on the other side of the family, but she'll take good care of it and enjoy it more than you. I'm just an old fool, and I don't know why God doesn't take me!"

Judy was speechless in amazement at the transformation in her aunt's attitude, but I jumped in to respond to her last sentence. "Aunt Diana, don't you realize why you are still here? Look what has happened to you in just twenty-four hours! You've changed from a demanding woman into a generous one, willing to sacrifice your own will. You went to God and asked for help. God gave it to you. You didn't like it very much, but you obeyed God. What an amazing amount of spiritual growth you have experienced in such a short time. Not only did you become more generous, but I'll bet you feel closer to God too!" Aunt Diana admitted that she did feel a stronger connection to God. "And that," I responded with glee, "is why you are still here: to grow into God's love!" She seemed to understand and said quietly, "I'll need to think about that a bit!"

Spiritual Needs of Persons with Dementia

As they pursue a mutual spiritual path, caregivers and care receivers have spiritual needs specific to their roles, but they also have some overlapping needs. Let's look first at the spiritual needs of care receivers—sick elders who are literally losing their sense of self and of their very lives. Here are some of their most frequently occurring and pressing needs:

1. Sick elders need to be assured that God loves them and that the dementia is not a punishment for some sin they committed earlier in their lives.

Many people still believe that God deliberately sends suffering to punish us if we have not been obedient. One of my patients, newly diagnosed with early Alzheimer's disease, firmly believed that God was angry with him because he had "given in" to impure thoughts. He was convinced that his disease, which caused him to lose his intellect and memory, was God's just punishment. Early religious training was hard to compete with, but when his pastor was informed of the man's intense distress and fear of God, he was somewhat able to convince my patient that God had long ago forgiven him and that a loving God would never send such punishment to God's beloved child.

2. Sick elders need to be allowed and encouraged to engage in religious and spiritual activities.

For a person who has attended religious services nearly every week of her life from childhood to old age, the inability to participate in a well-known order of service is painful. Researchers have shown that even for people with middle to advanced dementia, hearing familiar prayers and singing old, well-known hymns can bring them into a present reality, restoring "normalcy" even if only for a few seconds. All too often, caregivers are embarrassed to bring their loved ones to church, and often churches are not welcoming. So they stay home, watching services on television and feeling isolated. In addition, persons with dementia are often denied the sacrament of Communion. One pastor told me he had stopped offering his father Communion. When I asked why, he replied, "He doesn't understand what he is doing when he takes Communion." I responded, "Does anyone—even the most brilliant and theologically educated among us—ever totally understand the deep mystery of Communion?"

3. Sick elders need to prepare spiritually for death, and they may require competent help and pastoral care to accomplish this.

Alzheimer's disease and other dementias are terminal illnesses. A person may live a long time with the disease, but the loss of self is constant and unrelenting. Decisions need to be made as early as possible about what the person desires for end-of-life care, and health care providers can help with this. A time will come when the person can no longer ask God or loved ones for forgiveness, restore relationships, do a kind deed, pray, remember the good they have done, leave behind a spiritual legacy—a sharing of what was most important in their lives, or even intellectually realize there is a God and that they are God's beloved child. Because of the spiritual implications of this disease—loss of self-identity—the person who has been diagnosed with dementia needs to be informed of the implications of her diagnosis, and any questions she asks must be answered in all honesty.

Many caregivers instruct me, before our team's comprehensive evaluation: "Tell the doctor not to mention Alzheimer's. Don't tell my father he has dementia. This will only upset him. Just tell him his memory loss is normal for his age. Please give him some Aricept and tell him it's to help his memory. If a doctor says so, he will believe him." We do not honor this request. First of all, such a lie robs the person of his human, adult right to know the truth about himself and his condition. No one knows the secrets of another person's soul. No one, no matter how close, knows what spiritual issues need to be resolved before a person can die in peace. It is not so important to our team that the word *Alzheimer's* is stated, but that the person be told and helped to understand, to the extent of his ability, that his memory and ability to think and reason will progressively decline and that his illness will cause his death at some time in the future. All questions the patient asks should be answered gently but honestly; here also, pastoral care or spiritual guidance should be offered. Sometimes a pastor can help caregiver and receiver start the conversation that they will continue over time.

4. Sick elders need to know that they are loved and wanted and that "Blessed are the poor in spirit."

I have heard many caregivers make some variation of the following comment, right within earshot of their care receiver: "I've told my kids that if I ever get in this condition, they have to promise to put me out of my misery! I'm never going to allow this to happen to me and ruin my kids' lives! I'd rather be dead." They could just as well have said, "Pop (Mom), why don't you do us all a favor and just lie down and die?"

The need to love and be loved is one of the strongest of the four basic human needs. It is also a spiritual need. Even if a person can no longer express himself verbally, cannot demonstrate intellectual ability, and has no memory, at some level he can intuit meanings and feelings from the tone of voice and body language of people interacting with him. Infants (who have no memory or realization of who they are and don't know their mother's name) respond to a stressed, tense caregiver by mirroring their emotional state with crying and irritability. Similarly, people suffering from dementia have the ability to feel the emotions of those around them, particularly those who have been closest to them emotionally. "Reading" another person's emotional state is a skill learned very early in life and lost very late in the dementing process.

My friend Catherine visited her ninety-year-old mother, who suffered from blindness and dementia, daily. Some days her mother was agitated and confused and continually cried out, "Catherine, where is my Catherine?" even while Catherine was there. On other days she was calm and seemed more aware of her daughter. I asked Catherine to pay attention to her own emotional state when she visited and to keep a record of her moods for two weeks. What she found amazed her. On the days when she was relaxed and paying attention to her mother during the visit, her mother was fine. On the days when Catherine was in a hurry and stressed, in a low mood, or preoccupied with her own thoughts, her mother "acted out," as the staff labeled her behavior. In essence, her mother knew at some deep level that Catherine really wasn't present to her, even when she was sitting in the same room. Her wail, "Where is my Catherine?" reflected the truth of the situation.

Reflection

1. Think about a time when you had to receive help. How did it make you feel?

2. Think about a time when you gave help. How did it make you feel?

3. How well are your basic needs being met—are there any gaps?

4. How well are the basic needs of your care receiver being met? Are there any gaps?

5. What do you think about the idea that caregiving and care receiving can be a mutual spiritual path? How might it change the way you approach your role as caregiver?

4

SPIRITUAL NEEDS OF CAREGIVERS

Then the king will say to those at his right hand, "Come, you that are blessed by my Father, inherit the kingdom prepared for you from the foundation of the world; for I was hungry and you gave me food, I was thirsty and you gave me something to drink, I was a stranger and you welcomed me, I was naked and you gave me clothing, I was sick and you took care of me, I was in prison and you visited me. . . . Truly I tell you, just as you did it to one of the least of these who are members of my family, you did it to me."

—Matthew 25:34-36, 40

Care providers also have spiritual needs specific to their situation. Here are some of their most pressing and frequently occurring spiritual needs:

1. Caregivers need to know that no act of love is ever a waste of time for them or the one they are caring for. They need reassurance that caring is important spiritual work, even if it is demeaned by society.

Much of in-home care consists of small, humble actions that go unseen by others. Taking the person to the toilet; bathing, dressing, and grooming him; feeding him; listening to him ask the same question again and again; and looking after his physical health—all of these activities fill the caregiver's day, and she doesn't get much credit for it. Because caregiving doesn't increase the GNP, our society does not value the work of caring for persons with dementia. When society views caregiving as demeaning work, the caregiver is sometimes tempted to think she should be doing something "more important" in the world. The caregiver who gives up a good job or reduces her work hours is particularly susceptible to self-doubt. When you look at the situation through the eyes of secular Western society, it is hard to come up with a convincing argument for expending energy on a "lost cause," as some have crudely described it. Yet the Alzheimer's Disease Association estimates that the 8.4 billion hours of caregiver effort is worth $89 billion!

Because caregiving doesn't increase the gross national product, our society does not value the work of caring for persons with dementia.

If you envision caregiving as a mutual spiritual path, however, you can take encouragement and affirmation from Jesus himself. In Matthew 25:31-46 Jesus recognizes and praises those who have been the caregivers in society—those who fed the hungry, gave drink to the thirsty, welcomed the stranger, clothed the naked, cared for the sick, and visited those in prison. (Doesn't the person with dementia fall into all of these categories?) Jesus strongly asserts, "Truly I tell you, just as you did it to one of the least of these who are members of my family, you did it to me." And he promises the caregivers, "Come, you that are blessed by my Father, inherit the kingdom prepared for you from the foundation of the world."

2. Caregivers need to be reassured that their loved one's soul or spirit has not disappeared or become diseased.

One question I (Jane) am asked frequently is, "Where is my loved one's soul?" I answer, "Right where it always has been!" Richard and I firmly believe that the soul of a person with dementia does not deteriorate or go away. The intellect and memory may be lost, but the soul—a person's identity in the eyes of God—does not disappear. Who can say what the person hears, experiences, or intuits even in the latter stages of dementia? When you believe that the soul is still present, you interact with a person much more respectfully than if you think the soul is gone or destroyed and you are just caring for a diseased shell of a body. Some professional caregivers actually choose to care for persons in the last stages of dementia because they themselves experience a sense of the sacred, of God's presence, while caring for "the least of these." Their own spiritual need for closeness to God is met through the care they provide.

3. Caregivers need to know that their caregiving does not have to be (and could never be) perfect.

When someone feels bad or guilty because they have not lived up to their own, others', or even the care recipient's caregiving expectations, I ask, "If you have children, are you a perfect parent? Did you always do the right thing? Did your own mom or dad care for you perfectly all the time?" The answer is usually no. I remind them to be as forgiving of themselves as they are of their parents' caregiving imperfections.

4. Caregivers need to know that they are forgiven when they cannot love.

Love is not a feeling. It is an act of the will, and one chooses to love and to do loving acts—or not. Choosing to provide care is an act of love, especially if feelings of love and affection are not present. Since caregivers are imperfect human beings, sometimes they become stressed, tempers flare, and they say things to the care recipient that they later regret. Also, some caregivers find themselves caring for parents, siblings, or spouses who treated them badly or even abused them at an earlier time. Providing care for someone with whom you had a difficult relationship or by whom you were abused is a heroic act of love. Sometimes it is a blessing.

Christine, age sixty-seven, reluctantly and with some bitterness accepted the care of her eighty-nine-year-old father, who was in an advanced stage of a dementia related to alcoholism. She had not seen him in twenty years. When his second wife died, leaving him alone and suffering from memory loss and self-neglect, he was hospitalized for dehydration. The hospital staff tracked down Christine and insisted that she assume care. Neither she nor any of her seven siblings wanted to bother with him, because he had made their lives miserable as children due to his drinking, gambling, womanizing, and failure to provide for their care. Solely out of compassion for a stranger and feeling a heavy dose of guilt, Christine finally consented to take her father in. Prior to his move to her home, she came to me (Jane) for counseling to help her deal with the anger she felt toward him. Her struggle was, "How can I care for someone who made my life and the lives of my mother and siblings so miserable? The man is a stranger to me!" I listened to her anguish but didn't have an answer except to tell her to pay attention to the advice her "inner self" was giving her. I told her to keep in touch, but I didn't hear from her for months.

A few months later I saw her father's obituary in the newspaper and visited the funeral home. I found a very different Christine—a tired-looking but calm, peaceful, and even joyous person—a far cry from her earlier demeanor. She smiled as she came over to me and said, "I can't tell you how meaningful these past months have been, caring for Dad. Before he arrived, I decided to treat him as a stranger—as though he had not been a part of my past. I gave him a clean slate in my mind. This made it easier to physically care for him. He was grateful for any little thing I did for him. He didn't remember me, nor did he have any idea how miserable he made us years ago, but somehow that all disappeared. It was as if I was caring for Jesus. I've forgiven him, and I really think I have come to love him, in an odd way. The anger I've held on to for years is gone! My brothers and sisters never came around, and they will probably never be free of the burden of their anger. Caring for him was a blessing for me—we were blessings to each other."

5. Caregivers need to know that even if their loved one does not remember them, their soul/spirit is delighted by a visit or by the time the caregiver spends with them.

As a person loses the capacity to understand and use language, she relies increasingly on nonverbal signals to make sense of her environment. Most of our everyday communication consists of nonverbal communication, yet we don't pay too much attention to nonverbals because we are so word-oriented. But, just as in the case of Catherine's mother, the person's ability to "read" the caregiver's moods, feelings, and physical actions can be acute. She may become even more sensitive to the meaning of nonverbal behavior than the caregiver is! This is particularly true of love. If a caregiver spends intentional, loving time with the care receiver, even if the receiver doesn't recognize him/her, often the care receiver feels the love at some deep, soul level. If you choose to do an act of love, does it really matter whether the person recognizes you? If you can let go of the hurt of not being recognized, you can rest in the belief that no act of love is ever wasted, even though you may never see the effects.

6. Caregivers need to know that they can be the presence of God to their loved one, and that their presence is as important as any task they actually do for the person.

To be present to someone is to pay full attention to the whole person—to actions and feelings, as well as what the person says. Full attention means that one's own "brain chatter" does not interfere with listening to or being aware of the other person and what he or she is trying to communicate. Most of us have trouble paying attention well. We usually think about what we will say in response, or we may be preoccupied with other thoughts. Being completely present is a gift to the other person. It is a way of showing respect, of loving, and it has healing powers in itself. The basis of psychotherapy is to give the patient opportunity to be fully heard. The process of telling one's story to someone who listens wholeheartedly and whole-mindedly can transform.

The caregiver who has reenvisioned caregiving as a mutual spiritual path goes far beyond the act of listening. In John 14:23 Jesus promises, "Those who love me will keep my word, and my Father will love them, and we will come to them and make our home with them." If this is true, then every time the caregiver is present to the person he's caring for, he brings the presence of the Trinity to her. If the person with dementia is in the early stages and is familiar with the gospel, she may be able to grasp the idea of God's presence within. If she can, then it is possible for both caregiver and receiver to be God's presence to each other. Quiet time spent together or a meal eaten together may take on sacramental qualities. They will certainly be resting together in sacred time. In the later stages, just sitting with the person in the knowledge that God resides in both can make being together intensely meaningful.

7. Caregivers need to know that they may experience what is called "anticipatory grief"—grieving in advance of the person's death. This is normal.

When a loved one has been ill for a long time, as is usual in the case of dementia, the caregiver may find himself withdrawing from emotional attachment to the person—perhaps even wishing that the loved one would die. Most caregivers feel very guilty about these feelings and hide them from others, believing that they are betraying their loved one. Beginning the grieving process in advance is not a betrayal of the loved one; it is a normal process that some people inadvertently experience. The key to successful anticipatory grieving is to share the feelings of distancing with a pastor or friend. Being able to unburden oneself of uncomfortable feelings can enable the caregiver to protect the care receiver from feeling unloved or abandoned.

8. Caregivers need to know that they too are God's beloved and that God wants them to rest and have joy, and care for themselves.

Here's the part where we talk about how important it is for caregivers to take care of themselves and have a life they can call their own! Most caregivers resent hearing this message, especially if it is coming from someone who has never lived with a person who has dementia. Their usual response is, "They have no idea what it is like—she follows me everywhere, even to the bathroom. I have no privacy at all! And she roams the house at night, so I can't even get a decent night's sleep. I wake up exhausted every morning!" The counterargument typically becomes, "If you don't take care of yourself, you may get sick and die before your loved one," as if the only reason for keeping oneself well and alive is to be able take care of someone else.

It is true that caregivers need to take care of themselves—even the airlines tell parents to put on their own oxygen masks before putting masks on their children in the event of a malfunctioning plane. But staying alive just to take care of another is hardly an energizing motivation for self-care. God loves us and cares for our well-being just as much as God cares for our loved one. And God does not want us to be constantly depressed, exhausted, sad, and ill for the sake of someone else. Jesus told us that he came to give us abundant life. This means abundant life in every circumstance. There are ways unique to caregiving that can help create a life-giving space, a shelter for the body, mind, and spirit. Part of the process of envisioning caregiving as a spiritual path is finding and using these shelters.

Shelters for the Caregiver's Spirit

The following "shelters" are suggestions that may enable you to transform caregiving into a spiritual path—or to continue seeing your caregiving as a way to deepen your relationship with God. You may already practice some spiritual discipline, such as prayer, meditation, or spiritual reading. Continue to use whatever you find helpful. Sometimes, though, a practice you once used no longer helps or won't fit into your schedule. Consider the following ideas.

A Place of Refuge

As a teenager, I (Jane) learned to escape from the chaos of my family life by hiding in my parents' car. Even though I had my own room, it wasn't far enough away to shelter me from my father's terminal cancer and my mother's kidney disease and constant worry. Taking a walk often required too much effort, and I couldn't be away too long, so I'd slip out to the garage and get into the backseat of the car, close my eyes, and visualize what I wanted my future to be like. The car was my personal cave, my hermitage—a quiet, hidden place where I lived my own life. I stayed just long enough to find myself and gather up a bit of hope, maybe ten or fifteen minutes, rarely longer. I always emerged in a better mood than when I had entered, and I knew I could endure my parents' illnesses for one more day. After they died, I went to live with my high school teachers and their families. Because I didn't want to burden them with my grief and teenage moods, my car remained my shelter, my safe place. I never drove very far—just to a lovely spot on the bank of the Taunton River where it was safe for me to cry out loud or try to figure out what I wanted to wear for the senior prom. To this day, when work becomes chaotic, I go out to the parking lot and sit for a bit. It always works.

The first shelter you might consider finding, as a caregiver on a spiritual path, is a symbolic hermitage— a nurturing physical place where body, mind, and soul can be reunited. It's fairly easy to find if you don't live with the person you are caring for. You might try your car if your own home doesn't easily allow you a place for spiritual rest and re-creation. Some other possibilities are a church during the weekday, a lovely spot in nature, a library, a coffee shop if you are energized by being with people, or even your own clothes closet. The bathtub works too, if you can rely on privacy. However, finding privacy can be a challenge if you live in the same space with your loved one. People with dementia often won't let their caregiver out of their sight and even follow them to the bathroom. Once again, the car might be the place to escape for a while, if the loved one takes a nap or if an aide comes in to bathe him or a sitter comes for an hour or two to keep her company. The good thing about the car is that you can take a nap in it! (By the way, a sitter is to an adult as a nanny is to a child—very helpful. And worth the expense, if you can afford it. If not, is there a service you can offer someone in exchange for an hour of sitting one or two times per week? Ironing, mending, cooking a meal?)

Soul-Quiet

I could call this *prayer, meditation, centering,* or a *mindful practice*, but so much baggage, so many presuppositions go with these terms that I will use *soul-quiet* instead. You may have tried a number of these methods and failed, so I won't add another opportunity for failure. If you have a favorite one that works for you, go ahead and use it. If not, try practicing a way of attending to your life that Thomas Merton, the Trappist monk from The Abbey of Gethsemani in Kentucky, taught: "Now Here This." Let's explore the meaning of "Now Here This."

Practicing "now" means that you realize that the only moment you have is this moment—yesterday is gone, and tomorrow has not yet come—so don't be anxious about them. Be present to the present moment in your mind. You may feel tempted to take refuge in remembering past good times or anticipating a better future. These fantasies actually make us feel worse; they create a sense of loss because they don't exist right now.

Practicing "here" means that you realize that you are in this place and nowhere else. Place your consciousness in the physical space you are in. So often we visualize ourselves living in other places, either past or future—our minds are elsewhere so much! This is really a challenge when you are tempted to escape into an imaginary life elsewhere to find refuge. "Here" means paying attention to the space you are in right now—what it looks like, feels, smells, sounds, and even tastes like. Be present to your location.

Practicing "this" means that you place your attention on whatever activity you are engaged in right now. Try not to multitask; research shows that when you multitask, you use only a portion of the brain, and this can cause stress. Place your whole consciousness on the bath you are giving, the meal you are making, or the bed you are changing—without thinking judgmental thoughts about them. Just pay attention to what you are doing now.

Try not to multitask; research shows that when you multitask, you use only a portion of the brain, and this can cause stress.

When you are in the caregiving situation with all its mundane, strenuous, or boring requirements, this way of soul-quieting may sound like the antithesis of what you want to do—you'd rather remember the past good times or imagine a better future, slip through today, and be doing something different now. If you try it, however, you may be amazed at how peaceful you feel. Remember my story of visiting my mother-in-law and brushing her hair? I was practicing "Now Here This" without realizing it. This technique seems to expand the understanding of time, creating serenity in a stressful life.

A Spiritual Counselor

I recommend finding a spiritual director, guide, or counselor to help you on the spiritual path. There are many names for this kind of person (who does not need to be an ordained minister), including soul tender, spiritual companion, spiritual friend, *anam cara*, and so forth. Pastors of churches are often too busy and may not be trained for or comfortable with this kind of ministry. If you find someone who is willing to be your spiritual director/companion, share with that person your desire to reenvision your caregiving as a mutual spiritual path, and ask for his or her ideas and spiritual wisdom. This person can help you open doors to your soul that you never knew existed. A spiritual counselor is not a therapist and does not deal with psychological pathology. Rather, she helps you view and live your life in the context of your yearning for God. Most spiritual counselors see their clients once a month and, if they charge a fee, it is usually much less than that of a therapist. You can find trained spiritual directors through Spiritual Directors International (see www.sdiworld.org).

The Promise of the Resurrected Body

We don't pay much attention to the promise that ultimately we will have resurrected bodies and live in God's kingdom "on earth as it is in heaven" (Matt. 6:10). Yet this promise—the "resurrection of the dead, and the life of the world to come"—is part of our creed, words we proclaim as a matter of our faith. While you may not have thought much about this promise, it can be a source of enormous hope. The knowledge that dementia will not have the final word, that ultimately you and your beloved will leave behind careworn, earthly bodies and diseased minds and be reunited once again in your perfected, spiritual, resurrected bodies can powerfully shelter you from hopelessness and despair.

You can cling to this promise and know that whatever happens in this life to wear away our human identity, you will have yourselves back and will be happily together in God's good time. Bishop N. T. Wright's book, *Surprised by Hope: Rethinking Heaven, the Resurrection, and the Mission of the Church*, is a wonderful source of recent thought about the promise of our resurrection from the dead, and can offer caregivers a renewal of hope in this promised gift.

The above ideas are basic suggestions for developing a spiritual path. In a later chapter we will discuss ways you can walk together on this path with the person for whom you are caring.

Reflection

1. Have you ever felt that any of your caregiving tasks were a waste of time and energy? If so, which ones?

2. What are your spiritual needs? Which ones seem most pressing at this time?

3. Do you have a spiritual friend with whom you can open your heart about your caregiving experience? If not, think about individuals you know who might help in this capacity, or visit the Spiritual Directors International Web site: www.sdiworld.org.

4. Have you and the person for whom you are caring ever been on a mutual spiritual path? What are your barriers to engaging on this path?

5

SPIRITUAL CARE IN MEMORY CARE FACILITIES

Just then a Canaanite woman from that region came out and started shouting, "Have mercy on me, Lord, Son of David; my daughter is tormented by a demon." But he did not answer her at all. And his disciples came and urged him, saying, "Send her away, for she keeps shouting after us." He answered, "I was sent only to the lost sheep of the house of Israel." But she came and knelt before him, saying, "Lord, help me." He answered, "It is not fair to take the children's food and throw it to the dogs." She said, "Yes, Lord, yet even the dogs eat the crumbs that fall from their master's table." Then Jesus answered her, "Woman, great is your faith! Let it be done for you as you ask." And her daughter was healed instantly.

—Matthew 15:22-28

The story of the Canaanite woman and her request for the healing of her sick daughter has always baffled me (Richard). This woman, desperate for help, came to Jesus believing he could make her daughter well. At first, in a highly uncharacteristic response to human need, Jesus seemingly ignored her. No doubt the woman made the disciples nervous, especially since she was an outsider. They pleaded with Jesus to send her away. Jesus said to the woman, "It is not fair to take the children's food and throw it to the dogs," referring to all other groups outside Judaism. Jesus did not use the customary word for dog, but the diminutive word that describes a household pet or puppy. Clinging to the last shred of faith she possessed, the woman said, "Yes, Lord, yet even the dogs eat the crumbs that fall from their masters' table." Just the crumbs of kindness were all she asked for. Jesus was so moved by her persistent faith that he healed her daughter. In a genuine sense, the outsider had more faith than the religious disciples.

Communication Is Necessary for Relationships

People with dementia are often like that woman. At times their spiritual needs are not met by the church or even their families. These persons remain unseen, hidden at home or behind locked doors, and avoided by the church. All they ask for is crumbs of our time and presence, as they want more than just physical care.

We need to recognize that human life, including that of people with dementia, is grounded in relationships. Making and maintaining relationships with others is an important part of our humanity. Human beings are diminished when they remain in isolation or are merely treated as bodies needing medical attention. Human beings are more than body or brain, more than memory and rational capacity. They have another dimension: that of the soul or spirit, so often neglected in our hyper-cognitive society. Since the soul still lives in the person with dementia, that person's spirituality seeks meaning through relationships. We cannot be in relationship with another if we are not in communication with them. That is why communication with people with dementia is so essential if we are to be in relationship with them.

When I (Richard) began to do pastoral care with persons suffering from dementia, I confess I was extremely nervous and made many mistakes. After training and experience, I knew that the person with dementia is largely dependent on the efforts of others to make and maintain a relationship. But I was unsure of how to speak to people who rarely spoke or who would never know their name or mine. They sat and stared at me. Their minds were like a dense forest of neurons in which a kind of "neurological kudzu" had begun to destroy the lines of communication, until eventually nothing would remain.

One afternoon, as I tried to strike up a conversation with a woman who had dementia, she looked at me and said, "Talk to me. I'm still in here." I will never forget her words. She was simply asking for crumbs of healing, like the Canaanite woman. That woman's plea was a gift of the Spirit, used to open my eyes and heart to her. Gently I said to this woman, "I will talk with you. What can I be for you?" She said, "I want to go home." I knew enough not to say, "This is your home," which would only make her even more confused and agitated. So I said, "I understand you have a lovely home. Tell me about it." For several minutes she described her home in detail. I listened, and when she talked about her garden, I asked her if she would like to take a walk in the garden. She agreed. So we strolled through the garden in the terrace; in her mind, she was at home in her garden, and she was ever so happy.

I began to realize the reality-orientation approach, which I had used in nursing homes as a chaplain, was no longer relevant to persons with dementia. Trying to force our reality on them (the month, day of the week, the weather, the next holiday) is simply the wrong approach. These persons are living in their own time and place, and it is not the present, but the past.

One of our residents had to move to a skilled care facility. Her husband visited her faithfully at 5:30 p.m. every day. His wife, still living in the past, always expected him to be home at that hour, because that was the time he had always come home from work. A nursing assistant who was still locked into the reality-orientation approach, told the husband to visit only once a week. She said, "Your wife has to get adjusted to her new home." He complied with this demand, and when he didn't appear at the usual time, his wife became extremely agitated and anxious.

What matters to persons with dementia is having someone to listen with heart and soul, offering unconditional love. We need to enter their world. We never correct or contradict what they say or do. We must realize that occasional visits do not stimulate relationships. We must win our loved ones' trust before they will open up. So, the real answer is patient, persistent visitation. The more we are with our loved ones, the more we realize there is a spiritual dimension we can reach, and likewise, they can touch us. Even as the mind is gone and the body withers, they are "still there," with a valuable gift of their spirit they offer to those who love and care for them.

The more we are with our loved ones, the more we realize there is a spiritual dimension we can reach, and likewise, they can touch us.

Since I learned to depart from the reality-orientation approach, I have taken many wonderful journeys into the past. I remember Mildred, whose mind was living in 1942. She took me to wonderful places. We went to USO dances and said farewell to many soldiers who were being shipped overseas. There was one special soldier she mentioned with tears in her eyes. "He never came home," she said. Her past became her present, and mine too.

I sat with Jane in her room in our memory care unit. But she was elsewhere, sitting on her porch in a southern mansion, sipping tea. Her mind rolled back to the days of magnolias and servants. She called a servant for iced tea for us to drink. I motioned for a nursing assistant to bring us some tea, and when she did, Jane began to sing "Carry Me Back to Old Virginny" and "Tea for Two." I joined in and was right with her. When I left her room, she was still singing. Normally Jane rarely spoke more than a few words.

Through years of patient listening and entering their world, I have received the gift of these wonderful souls opening their inner selves to me.

Metaphors of Communication

The late Tom Kitwood used the image of a tennis coach in teaching how to communicate with people suffering from dementia. He compared the caregiver to a tennis coach who is able to keep a volley going with a beginning player. The coach lobs a ball across the net, and then wherever the player hits the ball, the coach somehow manages to reach it and return it. But he returns it in such a way that they are able to keep the volley going. The coach does not smash the ball across the net to score a point. Rather, he returns the ball gently so the other person can reach it and, with encouragement, hit it back over the net again. Likewise, when we attempt conversation with a person who has dementia, we can learn ways to keep the conversation open and allow the person to respond. After many visits, that person may become the coach and initiate the volley, and we simply return it to them.

Another helpful image is that of a whisperer. In the book *The Horse Whisperer* by Nicholas Evans, Tom Booker used his voice to calm wild horses, and his touch to heal broken spirits. The horse whisperer entered the world of the horse gently and lovingly and learned the horse from the inside out.

Stories about Communicating with Persons with Dementia

The following examples of communicating with people with dementia emerged from my years of listening to them and trying to live in their world and grasp their language. Trained in pastoral care to do verbatim (word-for-word) accounts of an interpersonal interaction, I would often go into an empty room and make notes of what I heard. It was like learning a new language, attempting to grasp what the person with dementia was trying to express with words or body language. After a while I began writing down some of their speech because I believed it was a way of affirming them. When I wrote down what they said, it made them feel that what they said was important.

A woman told me, "Talking about myself helps me get things straight. I talk a lot, and I didn't know if you would understand me, because you live on the other side. But when you write down what I say, you might find out what I am saying." She went on, "I'm glad you're writing it down, because when I say it to myself, it is gone." From then on, if a person was talkative, I had no hesitancy about writing down what he or she said.

On one occasion I hurried from listening to people with dementia to a Spanish class. This class was taught by a former high school Spanish teacher, and ten of us from ages seventy-nine to ninety-seven were trying to master a new language. I realized that I was actually taking two foreign language classes, Spanish and the language of persons with dementia.

It took me long hours to "hear" what people with dementia were saying. In one of my first interviews, a woman in a wheelchair kept crying, "I want my jewels." I thought that perhaps someone had stolen some of her jewelry. I began to listen more carefully, and she went on to say, "He was always cheating on me, and I just know he is having an affair right now, that Jules!" Later I realized what she meant. Her husband was Jules, and she wanted him, not her jewels. On another occasion a resident kept saying, "I itch. I itch," and wet her pants. "I itch" meant she had to go to the bathroom.

I recall a distraught woman whose husband came to see her, and she began screaming, "This is not my husband. My husband is only twenty-three. Get this man out of my room!" Instead of forcing reality on her by insisting that this was her husband, I softly said, "Yes, dear, this man just came to the wrong room. I'll try to find your husband." In a matter of moments she forgot the whole scenario, but her husband was visibly upset.

One of the most repeated phrases from people in locked memory care units is, "I want to go home. Take me home." What they are saying can be interpreted in two ways. The mistake some people make is to say, "This is your home," which makes the person more agitated. They may mean the home from which they moved or their childhood home. If so, you might ask them to tell you about their home.

However, they may mean that they want to go home to God. Gert had progressed through all the stages of

Alzheimer's disease. When she lived in senior apartments, I often asked how she was, and she would reply, "I'm still vertical." Later, when she went to personal care and had to use a walker, she would tell me, "I'm still breathing." Finally, as she languished in the memory care unit, all she said was, "I want to go home." She was ready to die, and not long after that, her spirit passed to the next world.

Once a lady clutched a doll, believing it was her baby. When I spoke to her, she said, "My baby needs to be baptized." Without hesitation I got a bowl of water, asked two nursing assistants to be witnesses, and proceeded to baptize the doll. The woman was so happy and said, "I just wish my husband could have been here. But he is away on a trip." Her husband had died twenty years before.

That experience reminded me of a story a priest told. He was visiting Kathleen, one of his parishioners, who sat quietly in a wheelchair. He said hello, but she seemed confused and didn't recognize him as her priest, even though he wore a clerical collar and a large cross. Suddenly she pounded the chair and screamed, "Why isn't someone doing something for that baby? Why isn't someone taking care of her child?" At first the priest thought she was referring to a program on television, but he saw no baby there. He spied another resident sitting on the far side of the room, screaming, "I want my mama, I want my mama," but no one was responding to her. The priest told Kathleen he would go over and take care of that child crying for her mother.

Kathleen smiled and seemed relieved. So the priest went to comfort the other woman.

Occasionally, humorous things happen when you try to talk with persons with dementia. I never laughed at people but *with* them, and at times I laughed to myself as I left the facility. As a pastor, I was visiting the mother of a parishioner who lived in a skilled nursing facility. The woman looked at me and commented to her daughter, "Where did you pick up this jerk?" I had to stifle my laughter.

On another occasion in the memory-impaired unit, John spotted me, and, pointing to a woman across the room, he said, "Can you help me get a divorce from that woman?" I discounted the fact that they had been happily married for sixty-five years and replied, "Sure, I know several good divorce lawyers in town." That satisfied him.

In a matter of moments, his wife came over and said as she pointed to her husband, "See that man over there? I think he's cute. Can you perform a wedding for us?" "Sure," I replied. "I still have my license and can arrange that without any problem." I began to look for another resident to converse with and hoped they would forget what they had said. They did. I saw them later, and they were holding hands, but after that I overheard John say to his wife, "Let's elope," which alarmed one of the nursing assistants, because *elopement* was their code word when a resident tried to get out.

Mary went to see her husband, who had dementia. She found him strolling down the hall holding hands with another female resident. Mary told her husband to let go of the woman's hand and go with her. After all, she was his wife. The female resident responded, "His wife? You mean I've been living with him, and he never told me he was married?"

Stephan was angry when he had to be placed in the locked memory care facility. At first he memorized the code, and once, when the nurses were occupied, bolted out the door. The nurses followed, and he was quite combative, wildly waving his arms and fighting off the nursing aides. As he stumbled down the hall, by the grace of God, I was there. Stephan and I had a previous relationship before dementia scrambled his mind. Somehow he recognized me and came to me. I calmed and quieted him down and led him back behind the locked door. Some time later, I became his confidant and friend. One night as I visited the unit, he whispered to me, "Let's you and I get out of this prison." In his confused mind, he was living in a prison where his neural structures, which had taken a lifetime to build, had collapsed.

Softly he said, "I know a way out. See those steps back there? We can sneak past the guard while she is sleeping and get out of here." I didn't know what to say; I couldn't go along with his desire to escape. So I replied, "That's a clever plan we can follow some other time. But I love to hear you play your piano. Would you play some music for me?" Stephan smiled, for playing the piano was his greatest joy, and he sat down and played "The Way You Look Tonight."

In his book *Loving Your Parents When They Can No Longer Love You*, Terry D. Hargrave uses a powerful image to describe how people with dementia must feel. He writes, "The closest I can come to putting myself in the place of someone with this terrible disease is to imagine myself as a soldier caught in a battle I didn't choose and one from which I cannot escape. In this battle, every move I make, whether it's defensive or aggressive, results in a decreased capacity to fight—with no victory possible and death my only certainty."[1] That is what happened to Stephan. He never wanted to battle dementia, but he could not escape from it. As his disease progressed, he never mentioned his escape plan again, since he knew no escape was possible. Now, in the final throes of this disease that is killing his brain, he never plays the piano. He simply sits and stares at it and never says a word.

It may well be that many times people with dementia are not without spiritual awareness and are closer to God than we think. The poor, confused, out-of-his-mind man in Mark's story of Jesus and the Gerasene demoniac reminds me of this truth (5:1-20). He did not even know his name, and, because of his madness, society had exiled him to a cemetery, where he was restrained by chains. The man rushed straight toward Jesus and no one else. Jesus moved toward the demented man and asked his name, affirming his personhood. The man's identity was gone, but he still had a soul. Jesus accepted him with unconditional love and healed his sickness.

I remember Hazel, who was full of hostility and often bombarded me with curses and vile language. I let Hazel vent and usually just listened. One day she was sitting in a side parlor, beckoned to me, and said, "You're a priest. I want you to hear my confession." I wanted to tell her I wasn't a priest, but, taking liberties, I sat in front of her, and said, "My child, tell me your sins." She told me some of unresolved issues with her sister that had caused her a lot of remorse and pain. I listened and said, "My daughter, say ten Hail Marys and five Our Fathers, say the rosary, and you are forgiven." She left with a smile on her face.

Anyone can learn how to relate to people with dementia. A woman whose mother was in another care facility and who mastered the art of talking with her mother and other persons with dementia, visited our memory care facility impersonating Fanny Crosby, the renowned gospel songwriter. The residents listened intently and even began to sing along with some of the old hymns like "Blessed Assurance." Maureen looked at "Fanny" and said, " I know you. You ate chicken dinner with us last Sunday after church." "Fanny" replied, "I sure did. Your mother is such a great cook. I really enjoyed that meal." Maureen beamed as she basked in the joy of eating Sunday dinner with her family and this distinguished guest.

On another occasion, the activity assistant was reading to residents a story about a woman who had lived to be one hundred years old. Matilda blurted out, "I'm a hundred years old too." Without batting an eye, one of our volunteer caregivers responded, "Really? You surely look good for a woman of your age!" She validated her feelings without correcting her. (Matilda was eighty-seven.)

I was leading a group of persons with dementia, trying to trigger memories of their childhood, where they are now living. I asked them to name presidents they remembered from their lifetime. Some named Lincoln and Roosevelt, but Jean said, "I am really worried about what Mr. Hoover is doing to the country. He's ruining everything." Gently I replied, "You know, you may be right. If things continue the way they are going, we may be headed for a depression!" Others in the group, living in the year 1930–31, chimed in with their anxieties about survival. One man said, "I may be laid off at the steel mill when I get out of this hospital, but I can survive with my vegetable garden." When I left the group, I had to process the experience and began to worry that I was really living in 1930 now.

There are times when you have to enter a person's reality to keep the conversation flowing. Years ago, I visited Annie in a memory impairment unit. I didn't realize she had reached the later stage of Alzheimer's disease, and she didn't recognize me as her pastor. She looked at me and said, "I like our pastor, but I wish he'd come to see me more often." Without hesitation, I replied. "Well, Annie, when I see him, I'll tell him." I had to enter her reality and work lovingly within it.

As I left her room, a lady was walking down the hall, counting from 1 to 25, pausing after each number. I noticed she omitted number 22. I asked her why she was counting, and she said, 'I'm taking the roll of my class, and number 22 is absent today.'" Then I realized she was happy as a lark, back again in the little school-room where she taught.

Recently when I was visiting a resident with dementia, another resident begged me to give her a few minutes, while still another resident kept calling out, "Help me, help me, help me." I went over to Gerry, and she said, "Please, can you tell me what time my class begins? I have to go by my classroom and study my notes. I can't find them anywhere." I knew she was living fifty years ago when she taught elementary school children. I glanced at the table where she sat, and wisely the nurse had scribbled "9:00 a.m. tomorrow" on a piece of paper. I realized what that meant, so I said to Gerry, "Don't worry. Your class doesn't start until 9 o'clock tomorrow morning, so you can leave home early and get your notes." That satisfied her, and she calmed down.

On another occasion I was visiting a woman who had moved to a skilled nursing facility in Greensburg. When she saw me she exclaimed, "Son, you haven't been to see me in a long time." (She never had a son.) I went along with her and said, "Mom, forgive me for not visiting you the last few weeks. I've been on the road. But I am glad you are here now and getting good care." She replied, "Well, this is nice, much better than the last apartment." She had no idea who I was or where she was. But I stayed with her and went into her own world. She talked about her husband as if he were still living and was the chief of police in the town. She spoke of trips they were planning for his vacation, and I tried to relate to that. Her husband had been dead for twenty years.

I heard other stories like that one. One nurse told me a lady in her facility was always gesticulating with her hands. She read her life story and found out she was a stenographer. So the nurse gave her a pencil and a steno pad, and the woman moved around the room taking notes. I heard another story of a doctor with dementia who was deeply depressed. A wise nurse gave him a white coat and a chart so he could walk around observing other residents whom he thought were his patients.

Many people have trouble with the thought of entering someone else's reality rather than trying to reorient them to the caregiver's reality. In years past, the idea of "reality orientation" was quite popular, but it was discovered that attempts to reorient the person to everyday reality can be disturbing and cause emotional and behavioral distress. The concept of "validation therapy" was introduced by Naomi Feil as another way to communicate with cognitively impaired persons. In this approach, the caregiver goes into the person's own reality and works with her from that vantage point. This method has turned out to be much more effective and humane because it validates the person's own experience. The point is that either we go into their world in conversation or gently try to recover who they were and simulate that activity. That seems to be far better spiritual care than reading stories these persons may not grasp or playing games they do not understand.

I remember Harry, who still was able to talk but always in garbled, confused language. When I visited him in his room, he was mumbling about getting to work at the railroad station where he had been a dispatcher. I simply listened, never corrected him, and affirmed his need to go to work. After I left his room, I scribbled down a poem as if I were Harry, living forty years ago:

My mind feels like the old railroad station
and it's time to go to work.
I see trains passing through,
steam engines and flashing signs that lurk.
But the old station seems empty with its
musty benches, cobwebs, and swirling dust.
It's time to get up and go to work—I must.

I shared this poem with his family and got their permission to publish it.

Communication Without Words and at the Time of Dying

As the disease progresses into the later stages, people with dementia regress to their infancy period of life. They cannot communicate with words, and are helpless as a little baby; they must be fed, dressed, and toileted. At this time, even when they cannot express themselves effectively through words, they still can indicate pain through facial expressions (grimaces), gestures (pointing to their body), and with vocal sounds (groaning). At this time, attentiveness to their nonverbal signs and the power of touch is essential. Although we must never encroach on their personal space, many people at this stage welcome touch. They have lost their defenses and respond to the caregiver only if the caregiver is physically near them. By touching a person at this stage in the same way he or she was touched by loved ones as a child, the caregiver rekindles memories of childhood. I remember hearing a resident muttering "Mama, Mama" when a certified nursing assistant hugged him. Even when his speech was gone, the hug evoked one word. Many people value someone sitting with them at a table, holding their hands, or brushing their hair.

When death approaches, there are still ways to get in touch with the spirit of a dying person. Celtic lore speaks of a "thin place" between heaven and earth, where this world and the eternal world are interwoven. Often as a person dies, he or she sees relatives who have died. The space between the two worlds is very thin now, and friends from the eternal world come to escort a loved one home. Soon they will be welcomed at a great homecoming party in the Father's house.

In her book *Symphony of Spirits*, Deborah A. Forrest suggests that many people with dementia are "evolving angels," that they show how thin is the veil separating the spirit world from ours. As the end of this life approaches and their bodies are leaving this world, their spirit grows stronger, and often they talk to spirits on the other side. A few weeks before my sister died from lung cancer, she told me that she had seen our parents and grandparents on the other side. I heard a story from a chaplain who spent time with a dying woman who was nonresponsive. As he sat with her, holding her hand as her breathing slowed, he sang "Silent Night, Holy Night." Strange as it might sound, to sing a Christmas carol at such a time, the words became a prayer as she died.

> Silent night, holy night,
> all is calm, all is bright.
>
> . . . .
> sleep in heavenly peace.
> sleep in heavenly peace.

When Jesus faced his imminent death in the garden of Gethsemane, he took Peter, James, and John with him so he would not be alone. He asked them to "remain . . ., and stay awake," for he was deeply grieved, as his death was near. The full brunt of what the cup would cost him the next day filled his mind, for he knew that through his death he would bear all of human tragedy in his soul. Even Jesus needed the presence of his friends at that moment.

Nothing is more important when a person with dementia dies than family members sitting with them, holding their hands, and praying with them as their spirit leaves this world for the next. Witnessing death never is easy. Being with persons with dementia as they are dying brings back reminders of my losses—my parents, sister, and more friends than I can name. It also reminds me of my own mortality. But I have learned from these persons that when they are ready to make the transition from this world to the afterlife, they exhibit a touching vibrancy of spirit. I sat with Jeannie when she was near death. She could not speak, but when I sang to her, her face glowed, and at times she seemed to sing with me. I realized that though her mind was ravaged by dementia and her body near death, her spirit was vibrantly alive.

Often a dying person will suddenly sit up and say strange things. As my mother-in-law neared death, she propped herself up in bed and asked, "Am I dying?" and died minutes later. On another occasion, a dying woman rose from her bed and asked, "Where is Howard? Where is Howard?" There was no point in telling her that her husband had been dead for many years, so quietly I whispered to her, "Howard is very near you now."

I recall being with a family when their loved one was near death. His daughters kept pleading, "Daddy, don't die. We need you to stay with us." I took them aside and gently counseled them to give him permission to die. I told them to say, "It's okay to cross over to the other side, if that's what you want to do. I hear it's wonderful over there." When they said these words, their father's face lit up with a smile. Softly I quoted the words of scripture—"No eye has seen, nor ear heard, nor the human heart conceived, what God has prepared for those who love him" (1 Cor. 2:9) and "Do not let your hearts be troubled. Believe in God, believe also in me. In my Father's house there are many dwelling places"

(John 14:1-2) and "Yea, though I walk through the valley of the shadow of death, I will fear no evil: for thou art with me" (Ps. 23:4, KJV). In a twinkling of an eye he passed over to the other side.

Darkness Cannot Extinguish the Soul

Caregiving for persons with dementia is a mutual spiritual gift. We can offer them our loving, patient, and persistent presence through the long days and nights of this funeral that never ends until their last breath. But they too bless us. Hannah offers a beautiful smile, although she cannot speak. I remember a resident with dementia suddenly looking at me when I was leading a group, and exclaiming, "You do good work here." You never know when these persons will show their appreciation by smiling, looking at you with love, or trying to say "thank you." I never leave that place of haunted minds without feeling blessed by these people whom so many forget. Maureen had grown up on a farm, and every time she saw me, she would say, "I love you little, I love you big, I love you like a little pig." It took me a while to realize these were words of affirmation.

My favorite story about this mutual spiritual bond is that of Ben. This big man, often agitated, suffered from semantic dementia. When I regularly visited him in his corner room, he would speak only two words: "Who? What?" Once he interrupted a worship service by pounding on the piano and muttering, "What? What? What?" Some of the residents seemed afraid of him, so nurses led him back to his room. Ben fascinated me.

Why just those two words? I talked with his wife, who had grown weary of his confusion and the fact that he never recognized her or his daughter. Her visits had become few. I thought I had a clue about his use of those two words, and that was confirmed when his wife told me that he had been a writer for a local newspaper. She showed me a scrapbook of his well-expressed articles. One day I said to Ben, "You know, Ben, you and I have something in common—we both were newspaper writers." Without any hesitation, he stumbled toward the door and said as clear as a bell, "I have to go to the files to check a story I wrote." For one precious moment his words were lucid, and his past became a present moment of truth the fog had lifted from his mind, but soon the fog returned.

There is a sequel to the story about Ben. One quiet Saturday afternoon I was walking around the retirement community where I live. As I passed the secured unit, the silence was shattered by a deep voice saying, "You're wonderful."

I glanced toward the window of a room, and there stood Ben, looking out the window. Ben had spoken those words. He didn't know my name or his own, but there was something about my constant presence that made him realize someone cared. What an affirmation of unconditional love from a man who had dementia.

There are times when I feel sad and burdened when I sit with people with dementia. But then I remember Ben's words of affirmation for me. So I keep going back. No act of love is ever wasted. The light shines in the darkness, and the darkness cannot extinguish it.

I (Richard) wrote this poem after listening to a man with dementia.

Sometimes I see myself as a flickering candle
that will soon go out.
My mind used to be ablaze with light.
Now every day the flame burns dimly
and the candle grows smaller.
One day all that remains will be a short pillar of wax,
but the wick will still be able to be lit.

Reflection

1. How difficult is it for you to talk with your loved one who has dementia?

2. When your loved one cannot talk, what are some ways you can communicate?

3. Suppose your care receiver says, "I want to get out of here. I've got to take my mother to church." How might you respond?

4. Suppose you ask your mother who you are, and she replies, "I don't know. You are a nice-looking person. Since I was never married, I never had any children." What would be an appropriate response?

5. Your loved one is beyond language and reasoning. You believe he is still "in there." How can you communicate with him beyond words?

6. When have you been with someone near death who was in the "thin place," where heaven and earth intersect?

6

THAT ALL MAY WORSHIP

By the rivers of Babylon—
there we sat down and there we wept
when we remembered Zion . . .

. . . .

How could we sing the Lord's song
in a foreign land?
If I forget you, O Jerusalem,

. . . .

Let my tongue cling to the roof
of my mouth
if I do not remember you.

—Psalm 137:1, 4-6

Some of the Hebrew people were exiled to Babylon in 587 BCE. They sat by the banks of the river Chebar in absolute despair. Taken to a foreign country against their will, they were far away from their homes and their sacred place of worship, the Temple. The common understanding of God at that time was that God was a territorial God. Yahweh was the God who reigned in Judah, but beyond that territory, other gods reigned in other countries. The Hebrews wept bitterly when they learned that the Babylonians had scorched their Temple. They had much to grieve—the loss of their homes, their Temple, and even their God.

Some of their Babylonian captors taunted them by asking them to sing them one of their sacred songs. With broken hearts and hopeless dreams they cried, "How could we sing the Lord's song in a foreign land?" They could sing Yahweh's songs in the Temple at Jerusalem, but here, among strange people and foreign gods, their words of faith stuck in their throats.

In many ways, people with dementia are like those captives. They have been taken from their homes and churches, some against their will. Some are captives in locked units, granted for their own safety, but making them feel forlorn and abandoned. Like those Hebrew captives, they have a sense of being moved to a strange place. They are not sure they can worship God in a new place. They too at first found it hard to sing their hymns of faith without the words choking in their throats. They are trapped souls with their past gone, the present strange and foreboding, and their future bleak.

When I (Richard) first began leading worship behind those closed doors, I remembered Psalm 137 and wrote it from the perspective of a person with dementia:

> Behind those locked doors I sit and stare and weep
> when I remember my church.
> I hung my choir robe in the closet
> and turned in my hymnal.

Even when these people come and try to make me sing,
the words stick in my throat.
I don't even know those strange people
who demand that I sing their songs.
How can I sing the Lord's song in this strange place with
people I don't know sitting next to me?
I hear the words of one of my favorite songs:
"What a friend we have in Jesus . . ."
and smile when I hear those words I can't sing—
"Do thy friends despise,
forsake thee?"[1] Indeed!
And then I remember
when I sang those words
as a solo in my home church.
How could I forget my faith?
God has not left me.
God will never forsake me.
So, in my soul, I talk to God,
and God hears me.

When the Hebrew exiles remembered Jerusalem, their spirits rose and their faith was reborn. They could not forget Jerusalem; even in a foreign place, their worship remained their highest joy. Little did they know at that time that this exile in Babylon would become a new way of life. They would discover that they could experience God beyond the boundaries of Judah. Eventually new forms of worship would emerge, and synagogues would become focal places of their faith, now that their old place of worship, the Temple, had been lost.

Worship for people with dementia is crucial for their spiritual life. I like to think of the hand as an image for the spiritual life—five fingers represent worship and other spiritual disciplines; the palm holds all these together, representing spirituality. Is it possible that learning how to help persons with dementia experience God's presence beyond the confines of a church building may create new forms of worship for us?

Needed: Creative Design for Worship

Jane and I believe that the spirits of persons with dementia can be reached on some level in worship. Our souls can connect with theirs. However, their needs for worship are often unmet, or they are herded in like sheep and made to sit through worship services that they can't grasp or that do not relate to their needs, especially to those who are nonverbal and unable to understand words.

Then there are those who remain in their homes, cut off from their churches and denied the worship of God. Where is the church in all of this? Have we offered worship to all people? It is a scandal if people with dementia are denied the chance to participate in worship and to renew their experience with God and be united with God's people. These dear souls remind me of the lame man at the pool of Bethesda (John 5:1-15) who came every day to the pool for healing but was ignored. No one ever really "saw" him. Perhaps he had become used to his helpless state and may have even liked being sick, because of the possibility that some kind people would contribute to his physical needs. But Jesus, the Great Physician, knew the man needed help to be made whole. Walk into any memory care facility, and observe how many persons are like the man at the pool of Bethesda. Some may participate in activities; others do not. Caregivers provide physical care, but few take the time to interact with these people or touch their spirits.

Jane and I believe that Christ came so all people could worship God. When Jesus saw how the religion-ists of his day excluded Gentiles from worship in the Temple and turned it into a profiting business, he exploded with anger. Quoting the prophet Isaiah, he exclaimed, "My house shall be called a house of prayer for all the nations"(Mark 11:17). The religious men of his time thought only of their own profit, not of the spiritual needs of all people. They kept some of God's people out, so Jesus drove them out.

When some of the Pharisees criticized Jesus for not fasting like other religious people, Jesus said, "No one puts new wine into old wineskins; otherwise the wine will burst the skins, and the wine is lost, and so are the skins; but one puts new wine into fresh wineskins" (Mark 2:22). Jesus bypassed those with minds closed to his gospel and poured his new wine into fresh skins, those few who truly believed in him. People with dementia, so eager to keep their relationship with God, cannot do so with the old, traditional forms of worship. When their minds have been ravaged by dementia, they need creative styles of worship that focus on visual symbolism and tactile objects.

Bonded by Interactive Support Groups

Often persons with dementia do not have much opportunity for interaction with other residents in a facility. At times their interaction with people is limited to the physical care offered by caregivers, or to visits with family members. It seems a rare occurrence when persons with dementia interact with other residents with the same disease, unless they live in the community and attend an adult day-care program.

I began doing weekly group meetings with dementia residents over five years ago, and these meetings are a highlight of my life. The activity director helped me form the group, which at first was mainly comprised of early-stage Alzheimer's residents. But as some of these residents moved into the memory care unit, I began to incorporate them into the group. I try to keep the group small in number (from ten to twelve persons). I focus on cognitive stimulation and interaction between residents. We have even talked about Alzheimer's, and I try to respond to their concerns. I answer only those questions they ask about their disease.

During the group experience, I employ various memory triggers. One aid I use to help group members remember their stories is a booklet called *MemoryBio Photo Album and Journal* by Beth Sanders, which consists of thirty-five themes with 250 photos. Objects and ideas associated with the themes give the participants opportunity to see, hear, smell, and touch a memory. (For more information about this product, visit www.lifebio.com.)

The wonderful result of these small groups is the bond persons with early or mild dementia form with others suffering from the same brain disease. Rachel, after several weeks, said, "You know what? Being together here reminds me of when the disciples were in the boat and a storm came up and Jesus calmed the storm. We're all in the same boat here, and I know Jesus is present to bring us peace even when the storm rages around us."

Some professionals disapprove of such groups, believing either that support groups for persons with dementia are a waste of time or are meaningless without some activity, such as physical exercise or mental stimulation. However, from what I have observed, these support groups help persons bond with one another and give them a sense of belonging. They remind me of the early church's koinonia, in which the Christians had "all things in common." The sense of belonging to the same community enhances group members' worship.

Creative Worship for Persons with Dementia

I have found the following elements helpful in weekly worship services for persons with dementia:

1. Familiar music

2. Memory cues

3. Visual and tactile symbols with music

4. The sacrament of the Lord's Supper

5. A closing affirmation

The Power of Music

There is a saying among those of us who work with persons with dementia: "Music is the last thing to go." Some of our earliest experiences of God occur in childhood. We associate these experiences with hymns that were popular in our churches at that time. Church music has the power to evoke memories. Helen was eighty-six years old, suffering from Alzheimer's disease. She rarely spoke. Her short-term memory was around thirty seconds. While we were singing "Blessed Assurance," I noticed that she began to move her lips and then sing, clearly articulating the words. Caregivers were astonished to hear her sing. Apparently the music had reached beyond the dementia to her soul.

Music influences the motor center of the brain that responds directly to auditory rhythmic cues and does not require cognitive functioning. It allows caregivers and care receivers to connect with one another. Scripture records how the sweet songs of David became therapeutic for the dark moods and depression of King Saul. On several occasions David's songs lifted Saul's soul from depression when his mind was tormented by the burdens of being king of Israel.

Any kind of music can break down the walls of cognitive failure that hinder persons with dementia. Jack, in the last stages of dementia, sat listlessly in his room at the end of the hall. His daughter had brought his old record player to the room, hoping he would listen to some of his own records. She played some of Benny Goodman's music, and when Jack heard the music of the clarinet and horn, he began to keep time with the music, tapping his feet to the tune and even singing the melody of the song.

Memory Cues

In general, persons with dementia are intellectually impaired and may not be able to understand words or express themselves. However, certain memory cues can facilitate their understanding. The sign of the cross, a crucifix, or other visual objects remind them of their faith. A friend of mine made a wooden cross with the Greek letters Alpha and Omega carved on it. I place the cross on the piano before every worship service. In one service Jean asked, "I see the cross, but what are those strange letters on the cross?" I explained that they are Alpha and Omega, meaning that Christ is the first and the last, that he is with us at the beginning of life and at its end. She seemed to understand.

Well-known and beloved scriptures and prayers, such as the Twenty-third Psalm and the Lord's Prayer, seem to get through to persons with dementia. They probably memorized these words in childhood, hid them in their souls, and may even be able to speak some of the words. At times I have tried having them repeat the Apostles' Creed, with limited success. The use of uplifted hands in blessing and passing the peace are other ways to express faith beyond words. Sometimes I wear a stole to remind them of their minister or priest. It is amazing how persistent the memory for things said, done, or worn in churches over a lifetime can be.

Visual and Tactile Symbols with Music

I have found that being able to associate an object they can see or touch with old hymns becomes a powerful form of worship for people with dementia. Here are some of the most effective ways I have used music and symbols in worship.

- We sing "Turn Your Eyes upon Jesus" at every worship service. As we sing, I point to a picture of Jesus that was donated by the family of a former resident who died. At other times, I hold up Heinrich Hoffman's picture of Jesus in Gethsemane, which still can be found in many churches and which residents may associate with their childhood churches.

  Sometimes I actually move to one side of the room with the picture, and motion to the residents to turn their eyes toward the picture as we sing the first phrase, "Turn your eyes upon Jesus, look full in his wonderful face." Once I told the story of Peter walking on the water, emphasizing that as long as he kept his eyes on Jesus, he did not sink in the waves of the storm.

- "The Church in the Wildwood" ("There's a church in the valley by the wildwood . . .") is another song from their childhood that they love to sing. My friend who made the wooden cross also built a little brown wooden church with white shutters, a white door, and a steeple. I show everyone the little church and pass it around the group. Some of the residents finger the cross on the door or the windows.

When we sing "No spot is so dear to my child-hood as the little brown church in the vale," I pause and ask individuals, "Tell me about your church." Except for a few, they will begin talking about their childhood church, for that is where most of them are in the present moment. During one of these discussions one woman became distraught and said, "I forgot to bring my Bible today," just as she actually did going to her church of long ago.

- Another favorite hymn from the past is "Rock of Ages, Cleft for Me." We sing the first stanza and stop. I show them two rocks: one from the white cliffs of Dover, the other from the beach at Iona in Scotland. I pass the rocks from row to row. They touch the rocks, and I have no idea of what they sense. Then we sing once again "Rock of Ages, cleft for me, let me hide myself in thee." I tell them that often people of God hid behind rocks for shelter and safety. Some understand, while others just stare.

- When we sing "In the Garden," a perennial favorite, I direct their attention to the garden outside the worship center. One time I even had some roses to show them as we sang, "I come to the garden alone while the dew is still on the roses." I look into their eyes when we sing "And he walks with me, and he talks with me, and he tells me I am his own," and I sense God's presence in these people's hearts as they relive this song of their childhood. I walked over to one woman who was nearing the end of her life. I sang the words to her, and she reached out with her bony hands and grasped mine. Surely God did walk with her and talk with her in a way I cannot understand.

• Each autumn we sing "This Is My Father's World." At times I read Psalm 1 and show a large poster of the words of Ecclesiastes 3:1: "For everything there is a season, and a time for every matter under heaven." I show the worshipers different colors of leaves, symbolizing the changing seasons: green leaves, bright red leaves, and brown leaves suggest how the seasons of life change, and yet each one displays the glory of God. For other suggestions for worshiping through music and symbols, see Appendix 4.

• One of the favorite choruses we sing at the end of worship is "You Are Mine" by David Haas.

> Do not be afraid, I am with you.
> I have called you each by name,
> Come and follow me,
> I will bring you home.
> I love you and you are mine.

> Text copyright © 1991 by GIA Publications, Inc.; 7404 S. Mason Ave., Chicago, IL 60638; www.giamusic.com; or 800-442-1358. All rights reserved. Used by permission.

When we come to the line "I have called you each by name," the pianist pauses while I go around the room and say each person's name. I can't understand it, but the words of this chorus seem to reach each person's spirit.

Anyone who leads worship for persons with dementia needs to be creative and intentional about speaking to their hearts and souls when their cognitive functioning is either deficient or absent. My wife, Alice Ann, and I always have a closing ritual with those who attend worship. At times we pass the peace and move around the room to look at each person. We grasp their hands and say, "The peace of God be with you." Usually they respond in kind or smile. We hug when they seem receptive or place our hands on their shoulders.

A reading of the Gospels reveals how important the sense of touch was to Jesus. Scripture records many instances of Jesus touching people and of people trying to touch him. When Jesus touched the lepers, the blind, and the woman who touched the hem of his garment, healing and power were present in his touch. I am always aware of God's presence as we touch each person. Some of their responses are verbal, like "Thank you," or "God bless you." From my experiences with persons who suffer from dementia, that touch somehow evokes some kind of healing, though I am not sure what exactly has taken place.

One morning as I reflected on the worship service while sauntering down to my apartment on "the other side," I had these thoughts: *In twenty years, unless a cure is found, millions of baby boomers will have Alzheimer's or*

some form of dementia. If they are residents in care facili-
ties, what hymns will they sing? Will they still sing the old
hymns? Or will they sing more contemporary hymns like
"Lord of the Dance," "Here I Am, Lord," and "God of the
Sparrow, God of the Whale"? Or will they sing praise
choruses? Then I remembered an old hymn I learned as
a child, "Tell Me the Old, Old Story." Remembering
those precious people in that memory care place, some
of the words took on new meaning.

> Tell me the old, old story
> of unseen things above
> of Jesus and his glory,
> of Jesus and his love.
> Tell me the story simply,
> as to a little child,
> . . . .
> Tell me the story slowly,
> that I may take it in,
> . . . .
> tell me the story often,
> for I forget so soon;
> . . . .
> tell me the old, old story:
> "Christ Jesus makes thee whole."[2]

The Sacrament of the Lord's Supper

Some clergy will not give Holy Communion to persons
with dementia. They believe these persons do not
comprehend the meaning of the sacrament and have
no idea of what they are doing. In my (Richard's)
opinion, refusing to give them Communion denies the

gospel and the meaning of the sacrament. After all, the sacrament does not depend on us but on God. God offers grace unconditionally to all who will receive it.

The sacrament is a mystery. Life is best defined not by rational intelligence but by mystery. The mystery does not require our understanding but our participation with wonder at God's grace. I find that sense of wonder when the Lord's Supper is given to persons with dementia.

In addition, memory is not simply the mental recollection of the sacrament but also a lived connection with the past. Individuals with dementia may not recall when or where they took the sacrament in their past, but they sense God's presence through receiving the sacrament. To deny them this sacrament is to deprive them of the most important Presence available to them.

Careful preparation needs to be made in offering this sacrament to persons with dementia. We must be sure the residents do not choke when they swallow the bread. Use small pieces of bread or wafers. It is wise to always have a glass of water available. The sacrament should be given to each person individually, saying their name, as you say, "This is Christ's body, broken for you."

Expect the Unexpected

Here is one word of counsel for anyone leading worship for persons with dementia: expect the unexpected. Anything can happen.

Sometimes individuals will blurt out words that could disrupt the service—comments like, "Oh shut up!" or "I have to go to the toilet," or "It's too hot in here."

Dr. Dwyn Mounger tells the story of someone with Alzheimer's who wandered into a chapel in a nursing home where he was giving Communion. Before anyone could stop her, the confused and bewildered woman rushed to the holy table, and, with one sweep of her arms, knocked off the tray of Communion wine. There was a sickening noise as it hit the floor, and the tiny glasses fell out, spilling the wine into a great stream as it spread across the floor. Some attending the service gasped, while others displayed no concern.

If something like this happened at a service I was leading, I would tell the residents that this accident was a symbol of the death of Jesus. The spilled wine was a symbol of Christ's blood, given for us.

Another unexpected event during Communion happened when a distraught woman took the bread in her hand. She squeezed it and then dropped the crumbs on the floor. She was embarrassed, but I gently put another piece of bread in her mouth, and she was happy. We must give more than crumbs to people with dementia. They need the living bread of God, revealed in Jesus Christ. His broken body provides health and peace for their broken minds.

In a nursing home where I served as a chaplain, a guest minister's sermon was much too long for the residents. When he finally finished, he said, "I have really enjoyed being here. I would love to come back." One woman replied in a loud voice, "I sure hope not!"

Anna was in the last stages of Alzheimer's disease. For some time she had been unable to speak, and she usually remained fixated in her Geri-Chair. During a worship service she suddenly began to repeatedly say, "Angel of God, my guardian dear, to whom God commits me here. Ever this day be at my side, to light and guard, to rule and guide." I realized this was a prayer she had learned as a child in her Roman Catholic church. It had remained in her heart as she expressed her childhood faith.

I knew Ralph had been a circuit judge and now had severe dementia; he came to worship in a Geri-Chair and was usually quiet and composed. In the midst of singing "Rock of Ages, Cleft for Me," he began pounding his chair and shouting, "Let the court come to order. Let the court come to order." For one shining moment he was back in his courtroom, in charge of the proceedings and so proud of his control. I walked slowly to Ralph's chair, clasped his hand, and said, "Judge, the court is in order. Let the proceedings begin." He quieted down, and worship proceeded.

At another worship service we were singing "What a Friend We Have in Jesus" when Frank, sitting on the back row, suddenly began singing "Show Me the Way to Go Home" (The second line says, "I'm tired and I want to go to bed.") I stopped the singing of the hymn and listened as every single person in the room joined Frank in singing every word of "Show Me the Way to Go Home" from memory.

Later I surfed the Internet and discovered that the song was written by the pseudonymous Irving King in 1925. Most of the residents were teenagers or young adults when the song became popular in America. So, the song triggered happy memories of parties and celebration. How appropriate for worshiping a man of Galilee whose first miracle was performed at a wedding feast of Cana in Galilee, where he turned water into wine to keep the party going.

Ray Inscoe, director of pastoral care at Westminster Canterbury, a retirement community in Richmond, Virginia, shared a profound story from his experience. A resident who moved into the community told him that she had lost her faith and had become an atheist. She developed dementia and entered personal care. Ray noticed that she began to attend weekly Bible study and worship, where she demonstrated a vibrant faith. Her dementia had caused her to forget her doubts and unbelief and to return to the foundation of her childhood faith.

A Moment of Grace at Christmastime

One year on the Sunday before Christmas, a moment of dementia grace occurred. Although we have special designed worship services for people with dementia, the nursing staff usually brings some individuals with dementia to our weekly chapel service for senior living residents.

The guest minister for this particular Sunday spoke for some time without ever mentioning Advent or Christmas. Suddenly Ida, one of the persons with dementia, blurted out, "Hark! the herald angels sing, 'Glory to the newborn king!'" Some of the residents smiled, while a few snickered. I rejoiced, for it was a grace moment as Ida expressed the meaning of Christmas from the depths of her soul. She knew.

Resurrection Behind Closed Doors

One Easter I returned from the worship service at our church with all its pomp and pageantry. I had seen little children with happy faces, dressed in their Easter finest, clutching baskets of marshmallow chicks and chocolate bunnies. A vast array of shining white Easter lilies had adorned the chancel, and the minister was at his best. What a contrast that Easter afternoon was when my wife, Alice Ann, and I led worship in a locked memory care facility. Halfheartedly the residents sang the Easter songs from their hollow minds. You could feel the depression in the room. It seemed as if they were miles away from the meaning of Resurrection Day.

With heavy hearts, Alice Ann and I went from person to person, repeating the words of the early Christians. After we had said, "The Lord is risen," they were to say, "The Lord is risen indeed." Every single one of them struggled to repeat those words. One lady, who never spoke except for babbling noises of confusion, smiled, and from the depths of her soul, she said, "The Lord is risen indeed!" Her response was no mere recitation but a proclamation from her soul. Another woman could not say all the words, but she grasped our hands and muttered, "Indeed!"

Marc, whose brilliant life had faded into the darkness of dementia, looked at me with a glint in his eye and a smile from his soul, and said, "Yes!" That for me was the Resurrection, the yes in spite of the no's that dementia had brought to him in his locked existence.

The risen Lord was present in that place. Dementia may take away the brain and the body, but it cannot steal the soul. My mind returned to that first Easter evening when the disciples huddled in the upper room, bewildered by all the events of that morning. Luke described their feelings like this: "While in their joy they were disbelieving and still wondering" (24:41). The disciples had locked the doors in fear that those who had killed Jesus would try to kill his chief followers. But suddenly Jesus appeared in their midst, unhindered by walls and doors, and spoke the traditional Jewish greeting, "Peace be with you." Once again the risen Lord had come to people behind locked doors, made himself known, and given his peace.

Mutual Spiritual Practice

Sometimes the effort required to read scripture, pray together, or attend a service is just too much for individuals with dementia. This is especially true in the middle and later stages of the disease, when the person is increasingly confused and confined to the home or nursing home.

When this happens, there seem to be few options for mutual worship or spiritual practice. At times when the person seems lucid, try some of the following activities, which will also benefit you as the caregiver:

1. Listen together to a recording of well-known and well-loved hymns.

2. For Catholics: say the rosary together (many people whose dementia is far advanced can still remember the words to the Hail Mary and watch Mass on television (EWTN programming).

3. Keep the Christmas manger scene on display all year. Stamped in our earliest memories, these figures bring consolation.

4. Borrow some children's Bible story books with lots of large pictures. Persons with dementia can still relate to simple pictures long after they can no longer understand or follow TV or movies.

5. When the person you are caring for is silent and still, take time to rest during that moment in God. Practice deep breathing and imagine you are breathing in the comforting Spirit of God each time you inhale. When you exhale, imagine yourself breathing out the peace and love of God into the air surrounding your loved one.

6. Watch videos of nature scenes. They are usually accompanied by hymns or other lovely music. These videos have no plot, and they don't demand an intellectual response, as would a TV program, so they are likely to be enjoyed far into the dementing process.

7. Finally, there is a practice that I (Jane) teach and recommend—the ministry of dedicated suffering.

This practice is a response to three questions:

- How can we respond honestly and creatively to the challenge and pain of others?

- How can we caregivers live a satisfying and meaningful life while suffering from two sources of pain—that caused by watching our loved ones experience the ravages of dementia, and that caused by our own physical, emotional, or spiritual pain?

- How can we make meaning of our loved one's suffering, even when he or she may not be aware of it?

Just what is "dedicated suffering" and how does it work? First of all, it is a spiritual practice—an actual ministry—based on two powerful scripture passages. In Colossians 1:24, Paul asserts, "I am now rejoicing in my sufferings for your sake, and in my flesh I am completing what is lacking in Christ's afflictions for the sake of his body, that is, the church." In John 15:5, 7, Jesus states, "I am the vine, you are the branches. Those who abide in me and I in them bear much fruit, because apart from me you can do nothing. . . . If you abide in me, and my words abide in you, ask for whatever you wish, and it will be done for you."

Paul's enigmatic statement in the first scripture passage has often raised the questions, "Didn't Christ's death on the cross redeem us once and for all? Why does Paul talk about 'completing what is lacking in Christ's afflictions'—what could be lacking?" Paul is not saying that Christ's redemption isn't true and complete; rather, he is saying that the world is not perfect. This means that yes indeed, we are redeemed. But it also means that humanity has not completely experienced the effects of redemption. So, like Paul, we are called to be coworkers with Christ in his vineyard for the completion of his realm on earth. And Jesus tells us that as we do this work with him, as part of him, whatever we ask for the good of the work will be granted.

Based on these scriptures, a devotional practice called *redemptive suffering* developed over the years. It was commonly used by Catholics but is not frequently mentioned now, unfortunately. In this practice, people who are suffering from anything—whether a serious condition or just an irritating one—offer their sufferings to Jesus. In his compassion, he takes the suffering and transforms it into love for someone else. It is very much like intercessory prayer, when you ask Jesus to help someone else. A common complaint we hear from people who are in pain or suffering is that they can no longer pray—the suffering overwhelms their minds, and they just can't concentrate on praying. Their physical or emotional suffering may be so great that it prevents them from experiencing God's loving presence. This loss of the sense of God's presence in itself is another source of suffering! (This was Jesus' experience on the cross, when he asked his Father why he had abandoned him.)

When I (Jane) was four years old and confined to my bed for six months due to rheumatic fever, my mother (who didn't like whiny children) taught me to "offer up" my joint pain to Jesus for the benefit of others. I liked doing this and thought a great deal about the people I might be helping. It took my mind off my own situation and cut down on the whining! I've continued to dedicate my sufferings, small and large, throughout my life and have found that somehow this practice makes the suffering more bearable. Since I have been diagnosed with lymphoma, I have been helped by this practice of dedicating my suffering once again.

It occurred to me, after sharing my enthusiasm for redemptive suffering with a pastoral counselor who encourages hospitalized people to "offer up" their pain, that this practice might be helpful for people suffering from dementia and for their caregivers. I now call the practice *dedicated suffering* and have taught it to hundreds of people in nursing homes, churches, retreats, workshops, and even at a conference on spirituality and medicine at Johns Hopkins University a few years ago.

It is simple to "dedicate" your suffering for the good of someone else. If you are doing it as a caregiver alone, just imagine yourself taking your loved one's suffering, combining it with your own anguish, and offering it to Jesus. Ask Jesus to turn the suffering into his own love to be offered for your loved one or for someone else. That someone could be another member of your family, your pastor, a member of your congregation, another caregiver, or anyone in the entire world who is suffering. One caregiver I know checks the newspaper each day for a cause—a person or situation needing God's help. Once she decides on the cause, she offers the suffering that she and her mother with Alzheimer's are experiencing to Jesus for that person or situation. Another couple offers their suffering as a ministry of love for the growth of their church family. Still another couple offers their suffering for the sake of anyone in the congregation who is sick. When they do this, they feel that they are still active participants in the life of the church.

In the early stages of dementia, when the person is still able to understand the concept of prayer, you might want to introduce this practice as something you can do either together or alone. Introduce it by saying something like, "Let's not allow all the pain and suffering we're enduring to go to waste. The apostle Paul offered his suffering for the good of the church. Jesus said that anything we ask for his work in the world will be done. Let's take the suffering this disease causes us and offer it to Jesus. We can ask him to turn it into his love and help for someone. What person or persons do we want to be helped today?" You may do this practice after watching the nightly news, with all its stories of death and destruction. When you and your loved one together (or you alone, offering both of your sufferings) give your pain to Jesus for the well-being of others, you are actually engaged in a ministry just as powerful as the ministry of prayer. The world needs the ministry of dedicated suffering. This practice offers a way to stay connected to and concerned about what is happening in the outer world. It gives profound meaning (and even usefulness) to the seemingly useless suffering that dementia brings, and it can be a powerful devotional practice for a mutual spiritual path. (For more detailed information about dedicated suffering, see chapter 7 of my book *10 Gospel Promises for Later Life*.)

Reflection

1. When have you felt like a stranger or an outsider in church? Describe the circumstances.

2. Do you feel that persons with dementia who are kept from worship in their home churches feel that loss? What could local congregations do to help meet their need for worship?

3. If music provides a way to reach the souls of persons with dementia, what hymns or other sacred music would you suggest? What songs or hymns do you think will be important to you in your later years? What objects, pictures, or other sensory cues could be used to remind persons with dementia of their home churches?

4. What do you think about the concept of redemptive suffering? Would you willingly participate in this ministry with/for a loved one with dementia?

5. What obstacles stand in your way in regard to this practice?

7

WHERE IS THE CHURCH IN ALL OF THIS?

A man was going down from Jerusalem to Jericho, and fell into the hands of robbers, who . . . went away, leaving him half dead. Now by chance a priest was going down that road; and when he saw him, he passed by on the other side. So likewise a Levite, when he came to the place and saw him, passed by on the other side. But a Samaritan while traveling came near him; and when he saw him, he was moved with pity . . . and took care of him.

—Luke 10:30-34

I (Richard) have loved Jesus' parable of the good Samaritan most of my life. I was born in the Good Samaritan Hospital in Lexington, Kentucky, so this Gospel story has been a key one for my life and ministry. Jesus' parable was prompted by a question from a lawyer about what he must do to inherit eternal life. Jesus replied with a question: "What is written in the law?" The lawyer answered, "You shall love the Lord your God with all your heart, and with all your soul, and with all your strength, and with all your mind; and your neighbor as yourself." Jesus replied, "You have given the right answer; do this, and you will live." However, the shrewd lawyer wanted the commandment cut down to manageable size. So he inquired, "Who is my neighbor?" Jesus answered with this story of response to human need.

The religious leaders, a priest and a Levite, saw the man in need but passed by on the other side of the road. Well aware of the risks on the treacherous road from Jerusalem to Jericho, they decided that they were too busy doing religious acts of worship to get involved in the poor man's plight.

The Samaritan, a hated outsider, had no reason to help this poor man. He easily could have rationalized ignoring the man's plight by saying that after all, the man on the road was a Jew. But in Jesus' story, the Samaritan man displayed compassion by taking care of the injured man. He tended the man's wounds, placed him on his donkey, and took him to an inn where he could recover.

The lawyer got the point of the story. When Jesus asked, "Which of these three . . . was a neighbor?" he answered, "The one who showed him mercy." This story is a classic example of the fact that no act of love is ever wasted. The lawyer learned that any person in need is our neighbor, and we all live in a neighborhood of need as wide as God's heart.

Many people fail to realize that we are like the injured man on the roadside. We deny that we act like the religious leaders, putting our own safety and religion above human need. We like to think we are caregivers, doing something nice for the less fortunate among us, as the Samaritan did. But rarely do we identify with the man in the ditch. Until we realize our own vulnerability and weakness, we will bypass or patronize persons with dementia by sending them occasional cards and paying token visits.

The Neglect of Persons with Dementia by Church and Clergy

In my (Richard's) work with people with dementia and with nursing home residents, and from listening to chaplains in similar situations, I have found that the presence of clergy in long-term care facilities is rare. In my six years of volunteer work with people with Alzheimer's disease and other forms of dementia, I have seen the presence of only a few clergy, usually when death is imminent.

I struggle to find the reason for this neglect of God's children. I am convinced that one reason is that most clergy do not want to face their own mortality and vulnerability. People with dementia are like mirrors in which we see ourselves. Many clergy tell me they stay too busy with parish duties to visit their members with dementia. They are ordained to the ministry of Word and sacrament, yet they deny pastoral care to these members who need their ministry. They often feel it's a waste of time to visit people whose minds have disappeared, and who never show any improvement.

So, like the priest and Levite, the clergy reason that it is a better stewardship of time to be where their presence makes a difference. They also rationalize their absence by saying that probably only a few families in their parish are affected by this disease. (That will change in the next few years as congregations face an ever increasing number of persons and families affected by dementia.) Clergy tend to pass over Jesus' story of the shepherd who leaves the ninety and nine safely in the fold and searches for the one lost sheep (Luke 15:3-7). When Jesus commissioned Peter to "feed my sheep," he meant all persons with no exceptions. God loves each person as if there were only one to love.

Clergy do not differ from the general population in that until Alzheimer's or another form of dementia strikes home with a loved one or friend, they ignore it. Some congregations now train laypersons in lieu of clergy to carry on the ministry of visitation to persons with dementia.

Both clergy and their congregations tend to reflect the prevalent ageism of our society. We have not moved far from the ageism of Shakespeare when he wrote, "Youth is hot and bold, Age is weak and cold; . . . Age, I do abhor thee; Youth, I do adore thee."[1]

Ageism demeans and devalues older adults, and nowhere is this attitude more obvious than toward people with dementia. The church continues its relentless focus on youth ministry. Church leaders insist that we ensure the future of the church by reaching young people. It may be popular to say, "Our hope is in the next generation," but we must not forget that our hope is also in the past generation. In many mainline churches, older adults pay the bills, thus providing funding for the youth ministries!

Like the priest and Levite, the church passes by the reality that mainline Protestant congregations and most Jewish congregations are aging even faster than the general population. If clergy and congregations have trouble dealing with aging in general because of denial and fear of their own mortality, how much more is this true in regard to persons with dementia? Perhaps another reason for this denial by both clergy and congregations is the gnawing fear that they too may face the possibility that this brain disease will knock at their door.

There have been scattered attempts in various communities to offer education events on aging for clergy, but they have been sporadic and usually poorly attended. When I offer seminars on dementia for clergy, few, if any, clergypersons show up. If there is an answer to the crucial issue of training clergy, it must originate with theological schools.

The Neglect by Theological Seminaries

The real burden of responsibility for the clergy's neglect of persons with dementia belongs to seminaries. Because many seminaries fail to offer courses on aging and ministry to older adults, clergy can become immobilized by their lack of knowledge and skills in relating to their older parishioners.[2]

Since its beginning in 1974, the National Interfaith Coalition on Aging (NICA) has sought to help clergy and other professionals preparing for ministry occupations learn more about working with older persons. In the late 1970s, the NICA developed a program called Gerontology in Seminary Training (GIST). The aim of the GIST program was to help participants develop courses on ministry to the elderly that seminaries could incorporate in their curriculum for students preparing for professional ministry. Among the participants were fifty-seven seminaries that belonged to the Association of Theological Schools (ATS).

In a followup effort in 2006 to determine whether courses initiated in the GIST program had continued, the Baylor University Center for Gerontological Studies surveyed the fifty-seven seminaries involved. The Baylor study found that thirty, or 52.6 percent, of the seminaries still list on their Web site at least one course in gerontology. The study also determined that only two seminaries, Luther Seminary in St. Paul, Minnesota, and New Orleans Baptist Theological Seminary, offered courses on aging. The Baylor study further revealed that only 26.7 percent of ATS seminaries (an association of 210 seminaries) offer any kind of course on the needs of older adults. The study concluded, "From this brief review of seminary education, it is evident that *fewer than thirty percent* of our seminaries are equipping [future] ministers in older adult ministry."[3]

By the year 2030 there will be seventy-one million adults age sixty-five and over, accounting for about 20 percent of the U.S. population.[4] Today 30 percent of the members of historic and ecumenical churches (Presbyterians, Methodists, United Church of Christ, Lutherans, and Episcopalians) are sixty-five and older.[5] Despite these statistics, most mainline churches persist in youth-centered ministry, almost ignoring a unique ministry for the growing number of older members. As we have stated previously, unless a cure is found for Alzheimer's disease and other forms of dementia, soon there will be a staggering number of persons with these brain diseases, and clergy will be unprepared for ministry to this burgeoning population.

More and more older adults are turning to the church and its pastors for help with aging issues. This need is exacerbated by the number of retiring baby boomers, who will not be as passive as former generations in asking for help and answers, which most clergy are unprepared to offer. Usually older adults are referred to social agencies that provide some help but not in spirituality or spiritual caregiving.

Unfortunately, many seminary students have had minimal contact with older people, and even less contact with persons suffering from dementia. Jane and I contend that seminaries must become change agents and place greater emphasis on training clergy for older adult ministry. The few studies of mainline seminaries reveal that this needed change in focus is not happening.

Stephen Sapp and Henry Simmons have been long-time advocates of seminaries offering courses in aging. However, in an exchange of letters with me (Richard), both paint a dismal picture of change at mainline seminaries in the training of clergy in older adult ministry. Simmons, director of the Center for Aging at Union Theological Seminary/Presbyterian School of Christian Education in Richmond, Virginia, wrote, "I have offered a general Ministry with Older Adults course four times—and every time I got exactly one student. . . . It is a dismal, life-denying picture. Nothing to be cheered about."[6]

Stephen Sapp, dean of religion at the University of Miami in Florida, wrote, "As far as I know, virtually no theological schools are doing anything meaningful in preparing their students in gerontology, much less with regard to dementia specifically. . . . This is incredibly shortsighted given the age of the mainline denominations and the inevitable continuation of that trend."[7]

Dr. Richard Gentzler, director of the Center on Aging and Older Adult Ministry for the United Methodist Church, may be the only staff member for older adult ministry in any ecumenical or historic denomination. He reports that there is a smattering of courses on aging and the needs of an aging society in a few of the thirteen United Methodist seminaries, far too few to make an impact on future clergy.[8]

Future hope for change lies in adding courses to the seminary curriculum, as well as clinical pastoral education (CPE) courses in nursing homes and memory care facilities. Regarding the curriculum, seminaries are still locked into their focus on being graduate professional schools for academia. While we do not want to minimize the value of academic education, is there not also a place in pastoral care for courses that deal with people who are "out of their mind" but are still children of God? Jane and I hope so.

There is more hope for change in CPE courses with hands-on training and internships in memory care or skilled nursing facilities. Not only would such clinical training give seminary students vital connections with older people and those suffering from dementia, but also future ministers would discover the wealth of wisdom and spirituality that older people have available to share.

Cautious Optimism

1. Theological Seminaries

For years, Jane and I have felt like prophets crying in the wilderness about the need for ministry for older persons in general, and specifically for persons with dementia. We believe that all seminaries should offer courses in gerontology and pastoral care of older adults.

Some medical schools, aware of the burgeoning aging population in America, now require one full rotation in geriatric medicine for medical students and residents. This includes the latest research into dementia, its cause, and suggested medicines. Can theological seminaries afford to do any less?

2. Pastoral Care of Members in the Parish

If clergy are trained by seminaries, or if they will attend conferences on leading worship for and visiting their parish members with dementia, they will be equipped. Chapter 6 included suggestions for leading worship for persons with dementia.

Trained clergy can inspire their congregations to begin visitation programs and care groups for persons with dementia. The most important thing to remember is that these persons need continual presence, friendship, time, and listening.

As the incurable disease of dementia continues to strike more people in the new few years, I (Richard) believe clergy will become more intentional about visiting members and families who are dealing with dementia. It is not easy to be present to someone who will never get well but becomes progressively worse and loses reason and language. But like the prophet Ezekiel, who came to the exiles at Tel-Abib and sat there among them (Ezek. 2:15), clergy are called to "sit among" persons with dementia, who are exiles in a strange land which neither they nor the clergy can understand.

Congregational Responses

What can individual churches do to respond to the needs of persons with dementia and their caregivers? From my (Jane's) experience of working closely with churches of all denominations, I believe the following are key elements for a church's program to attend to the needs of caregivers and receivers. (This goes beyond but may include the senior adult group that may already be active in the church.)

1. Assessment—know who the caregivers and receivers are!

Churches can respond to needs in a number of ways. First, the pastoral staff needs to know who in the congregation has a dementing disease and/or who is a caregiver. The two don't necessarily coincide; the caregiver and receiver may not belong to the same church—or one may never have belonged to a faith community. One way to discover both is to send out a survey. This can be done as part of a general survey, which includes other issues, or it can be caregiver/receiver specific.

Another way to do this is to place a notice in the weekly church bulletin or monthly newsletter with a request like the following:

> Our church is trying to be responsive to the needs of persons with dementing diseases such as Alzheimer's and to the needs of their caregivers. First, we need to know who these persons are!
>
> • If you provide care to someone with Alzheimer's disease or another type of dementia, please notify the pastoral staff by calling the following number: [insert church's phone number].
>
> • If you know a church member who cares for someone with Alzheimer's or other dementia, or if you know a church member with dementia, please notify the pastoral staff. We need to know who they are so we can serve them. As soon as we know of a caregiver or care recipient, we will contact them to see how our church can help.
>
> Note: The need for care is greater than the need for privacy.

2. Visit regularly!

The next step is to make pastoral visits to the caregiver and/or recipient to assess needs. This can be done by the official pastoral staff, a parish nurse, or by a staff member and a volunteer. Many churches have Stephen Ministries; such visits would be an ideal outreach for these volunteers. Simply asking the open-ended question, "How can we be of help?" is a good way to begin. Frequently people are so overwhelmed by their situation that they can't even articulate their needs. The needs addressed do not necessarily have to be spiritual. The caregiver might want to know what community resources are available, when to use adult day-care centers, or when and how to place the person in a long-term care facility. Caregivers have many conflicting feelings about placing their loved ones in nursing homes—guilt, grief, anger, fear, and frustration, to name a few. Often caregivers promised years ago that they would never put a family member in a home. Now, when they can no longer care for the person at home, they feel tremendous guilt about breaking that promise. Pastoral care is vital in this circumstance.

Beyond assessment and provision of information, regular visitation is essential. The ability to provide needed information is valuable, but the essence of spiritual care comes from the very fact of the visit and the willingness of the visitor to take the time to listen. The therapeutic effect of being listened to is immeasurable. Caregivers are frequently isolated in their homes as they care for the person with dementia. They have no one with whom to share their anguish, to unburden themselves. This isolation causes much of the suffering that caregivers experience. Whoever visits brings the presence of God to the caregiver and receiver. The visitor is Christ's heart, ears, eyes, and hands. Visit regularly and often!

3. Educate the congregation.

Dementia, a terminal disease, is now the sixth cause of death in adults age sixty-five and over. It is so common that it affects many of us, even if we are not the primary caregivers. For example, grandchildren who once had close and loving relationships with a grandparent with dementia are often forgotten in the caregiving process. They may not understand why their granny doesn't know them any longer, or why Granddad is always so angry at them. Close friends whose company a couple has enjoyed for many years may withdraw because they don't know how to talk with the person with dementia. Church members may not know how to respond when a member with Alzheimer's starts to talk or sing out loud in the quiet part of the worship service. Pastors who have not been trained to care for persons with dementia, or who view them as no longer needing spiritual care, may avoid home visitation. The end result is that the caregiver and receiver are left alone to fend for themselves. A caregiving husband once said, "When my wife had her gallbladder out years ago, her church friends came around with casseroles and other goodies every day for a couple of weeks—until she was on her feet again. But when you have Alzheimer's, it goes on too long; people forget about you." Unfortunately, this situation is all too common.

What is the answer? One answer to the problem of avoidance is education of the entire congregation, including youth. People fear and withdraw from what they do not know. When they are given information and skills, they are more likely to be helpful—or at least be more understanding and more tolerant. Because dementia is so common and so many of our faith communities are filled with older adults (who are at a higher risk of developing dementia), the whole church needs to be informed of the facts and fallacies of dementia. A free, one-hour educational program or a series of lectures can be provided, with the whole congregation invited (and food served). Or, dementia can be the topic of presentations to many of the church organizations. A Sunday school class or a missions organization may invite a speaker with knowledge of dementia. The local Alzheimer's Disease and Related Disorders Association is an excellent source of speakers. Their presenters do not charge fees, and one of their primary missions is to educate the public about Alzheimer's and related dementing diseases. In addition, they often provide a lending library for caregivers and offer their own dementia workshops and lecture series. Most AD associations also have monthly educational sessions for caregivers and the general public. Churches should make use of this remarkable resource. Once people know about dementia, some of their fears will be allayed, and they will become more welcoming and responsive to members of the congregation who are affected by dementia. They may even learn ways to reduce their own risk of developing a dementing illness.

4. Offer respite.

One of the trials of caregiving is that it is a 24/7 experience. Some caregivers can't even get time alone in the bathroom! An excellent way to be of service to a caregiver is to offer to stay with the person with dementia while the caregiver takes a nap or goes to get a haircut, to church, or to a support group meeting. Sometimes the person with dementia will not stay with a hired aide he doesn't know but will be content to be in the care of someone from church, someone whose face he knows. Churches could develop "respite teams"—people willing to "sit" with the person to give the caregiver one or more hours of free time—or even time to go to a church service or Sunday school class. Caregivers often report that they would love to be able to go to church, but they can't leave their loved one. When this happens, they are cut off from an important source of support that could enable them to cope with their situation. Church provides for continuity of life both spiritually and socially for the caregiver. These supports are essential to caregiver health and well-being.

5. Offer transportation.

One of the difficulties of traveling to the physician's office is that the person with dementia may try to get out of the car or become restless and irritable. This puts both caregiver and receiver in danger. If someone else drives, however, the caregiver can give all of his attention to the receiver.

6. Offer opportunities to worship.

The ideal response to the person with dementia would be to incorporate him into the regular, traditional worship service. If that is not possible because the person's behavior is too disruptive to the rest of the congregation, the use of the "cry room" (a place where babies are taken) might be a solution. Another idea is to create a special monthly service designed specifically for caregivers and receivers and their extended family members. Emphasis on hymn singing and movement is more effective than a sermon, as Richard explained in the last chapter.

7. Offer pastoral counseling.

In the early stages of dementia, the person is trying to process the meaning of the disease. She may have pressing spiritual needs to discuss with a pastor. Issues of forgiveness and regret often emerge. Just because a person has the diagnosis of dementia does not mean that she can't reason and think abstractly. In the early stages of Alzheimer's, particularly, the memory and visuospatial skills are the areas primarily affected. The person can still make decisions about her life and can think about her life and spiritual needs.

Pastoral counseling should be made available to the caregiver for the entire duration of the loved one's illness. Dementia brings with it intense spiritual questions, such as "Why has God done this to us?" "Where is my husband's soul?" "I feel so guilty when I am cross with my wife!" "Am I a bad person to wish that this ordeal was over?" "I promised never to put my father in a nursing home, but I just can't care for him at home any longer. I know I must do it, but I feel so guilty, and I can't bear his anger at me!"

8. Be advocates.

One way to improve the plight of the person with dementia is to join the Alzheimer's Association's yearly "Memory Walk" to raise money for dementia research. Another way is to advocate at the level of local, state, and national government. Contacting legislators to support increased funding for research and resources is a way for people who can't do hands-on ministry to help. The active seniors group in the church could take on this kind of advocacy as its ministry.

In summary, the key message for churches facing the problem of dementia and its effects is "be available." Being welcoming, caring, interested, willing to listen, and willing to reassure the caregiver that the person with dementia is still loved by the congregation is a response to Jesus' statement, "Just as you did it to one of the least of these who are members of my family, you did it to me" (Matt. 25:40).

Conclusion

The comparison of persons with dementia to the Babylonian exiles is a powerful analogy. Care receivers and their caregivers are like the ancient Hebrews, trapped in a strange country. They have no choice about being separated from the mainstream of life. Persons with dementia, whether in care facilities or at home, feel cut off from life, and caregivers often feel the heavy burden of caregiving has disrupted their life. But there is more to the rest of the story.

Even as the Babylonian siege engines breached the walls of Jerusalem, Jeremiah negotiated to buy a field at Anathoth at a fair market price. It was an act of economic lunacy. Jeremiah himself had predicted that the Babylonians would capture the city and take its citizens into captivity. Why, then, this stupid act of buying land that soon would belong to his enemies? Jeremiah made a venture of faith and invested in the future. He believed that "houses and fields and vineyards shall again be bought in this land" (Jer. 32:15). In 539 BCE the exiles returned to their homes. God's promise was fulfilled after forty-eight years! The Hebrews learned that God had indeed done a new thing, provided a way in the wilderness, offered renewal of hope.

It may take another generation or more, but we believe that through our willingness to embrace this grave challenge, God will act on behalf of persons afflicted with dementia. Change comes slowly, but already we see signs of hope. God has not forsaken these exiles either. It is hard for caregivers to feel any hope. One daughter of a man with dementia told our support group, "I visit my father every day. When he has lucid moments, I want to cherish the memory that he knew me." Another member of our Alzheimer's support group said tearfully, "It's so hard. My whole life has been changed since my mother-in-law came to live with us. I know that no amount of my loving care can cure her. I just feel so helpless."

The question remains, "Where is the church in all of this?" But the deeper question is, "Where is God in all of this?" The church's responsibility is to answer the question of a ministry for persons with dementia and their caregivers. God has already answered that question. God never forsakes the weak and needy of any generation. God is present in the souls of people with dementia and with those who care for them. So, hope remains that even when love seems to be defeated, no act of love is ever wasted.

Reflection

1. If you are a caregiver, what questions would you ask your pastor about your situation?

2. If you are a clergyperson, what would you suggest to your seminary about offering continuing education courses in gerontology and pastoral care?

3. As a pastor, what can you do to energize your congregation to get involved in a ministry for caregivers?

4. If your church is not yet organized to help caregivers and receivers, what can you do to help?

Appendix 1

SUGGESTED READING

Barton, Julie, Marita Grudzen, and Ron Zielske. *Vital Connections in Long-Term Care: Spiritual Resources for Staff and Residents.* Towson, MD: Health Professions Press, 2003.

Bell, Virginia M., and David Troxel. *The Best Friends Approach to Alzheimer's Care.* Towson, MD: Health Professions Press, 2003.

Brackey, Jolene. *Creating Moments of Joy for the Person with Alzheimer's or Dementia.* 4th ed. West Lafayette, IN: Purdue University Press, 2007.

Bryden, Christine. *Dancing with Dementia: My Story of Living Positively with Dementia.* Philadelphia: Jessica Kingsley Publishers, 2005.

Coste, Joanne Koenig. *Learning to Speak Alzheimer's: A Groundbreaking Approach for Everyone Dealing with the Disease.* Boston: Houghton Mifflin Company, 2004.

DeBaggio, Thomas. *Losing My Mind: An Intimate Look at Life with Alzheimer's.* New York: Simon and Schuster, 2003.

Forrest, Deborah A., with Clint Richmond. *Symphony of Spirits: Encounters with the Spiritual Dimensions of Alzheimer's.* New York: St. Martin's Press, 2000.

Genova, Lisa. *Still Alice: A Novel.* New York: Pocket Books, 2007. [This is the best novel I (Richard) have read about Alzheimer's disease. The reader can view the surreal world of early-onset Alzheimer's disease from within that world.]

Gentzler, Richard H., Jr. *Aging and Ministry in the 21st Century: An Inquiry Approach*. Nashville: Discipleship Resources, 2008.

Goldsmith, Malcolm. *In a Strange Land: People with Dementia and the Local Church*. Southwell, Great Britain: 4M Publications, 2004.

Grollman, Earl A., and Kenneth S. Kosik. *When Someone You Love Has Alzheimer's: The Caregiver's Journey*. Boston: Beacon Press, 1996.

Hargrave, Terry. *Strength and Courage for Caregivers*. Grand Rapids, MI: Zondervan, 2008.

Keck, David. *Forgetting Whose We Are: Alzheimer's Disease and the Love of God*. Nashville: Abingdon Press, 1996.

Kessler, Lauren. *Dancing with Rose: Finding Life in the Land of Alzheimer's*. New York: Penguin Books, 2007.

Kitwood, Tom. *Dementia Reconsidered: The Person Comes First*. Philadelphia: Open University Press, 1997.

Knight, Bethany. *Blessed Are the Caregivers: A Daily Book of Comfort and Cheer*. Albuquerque: Hartman Publishing, 2001.

Mace, Nancy L., and Peter V. Rabins. *The 36-Hour Day: A Family Guide to Caring for People with Alzheimer's Disease, Other Dementias, and Memory Loss in Later Life*. 4th ed. Baltimore, MD.: Johns Hopkins University Press, 2007.

McKim, Donald K., ed. *God Never Forgets: Faith, Hope and Love and Alzheimer's Disease*. Louisville, KY: Westminster John Knox Press, 1997.

Morgan, Richard L. *Fire in the Soul: A Prayer Book for the Later Years*. Nashville: Upper Room Books, 2000.

Noonan, Nell E. *Not Alone: Encouragement for Caregivers*. Nashville: Upper Room Books, 2009.

Sapp, Stephen. *When Alzheimer's Disease Strikes*. Charlotte, NC: Desert Ministries, 2003.

Shamy, Eileen. *A Guide to the Spiritual Dimension of Care for People with Alzheimer's Disease and Related Dementias: More than Body, Brain, and Breath*. Philadelphia: Jessica Kingsley Publishers, 2003.

Thibault, Jane Marie. *A Deepening Love Affair: The Gift of God in Later Life*. Nashville: Upper Room Books, 1993.

Thibault, Jane Marie. *10 Gospel Promises for Later Life*. Nashville: Upper Room Books, 2004.

Whitehouse, Peter J., with Daniel George. *The Myth of Alzheimer's: What You Aren't Being Told About Today's Most Dreaded Diagnosis*. New York: St. Martin's Press, 2008.

Wright, Nicholas Thomas. *Surprised by Hope: Rethinking Heaven, the Resurrection, and the Mission of the Church*. New York: HarperCollins Publishers, 2008.

Yearwood, Mary Margaret Britton. *In Their Hearts: Inspirational Alzheimer's Stories*. Victoria, BC: Trafford Publishing, 2002.

Appendix 2

PSALM 139 FOR CAREGIVERS

O God, you know my heart,
    and only you understand how hard
    I have tried to care for my loved one.
You know that I hardly have time to sit down
    or care for myself;
you know the long hours I spend
    working and serving my loved one.
Only you know the depth of anger I feel
    toward my family for their lack of help,
and you know the harsh words I often speak
    to the one I love—even before I say them.
I find it hard to hear your gentle voice
    telling me to slow down,
    not to fall prey to anxiety,
    and to stop and rest in you.
You bless me even when I fail miserably,
    when I get down on myself,
    when I feel guilty for not doing enough.
Such understanding and grace are
    beyond my comprehension.
I can never get away from you;
    I cannot outlive your love.
If I have good days with my loved one,
    when they have flashes of recognition,
    you are there, celebrating with me.

If I sink down into the pits of despair
    when everything is going wrong,
    you are also there.
If I allow my mind to wander to more pleasant places,
    you are there.
When the darkness of being on call around the clock
    engulfs me and I want to scream,
    you stand beside me and calm me.
And when I am tempted to believe that
    all of this effort is wasted,
when I think I am wasting my life,
    caring for something that will never come to fruition,
    you hold me closest to your heart.
You know what it is like to experience
    dark nights of the soul.
Even though my loved one has this dreadful
    brain disease and no longer knows who I am,
I will still believe their soul is alive
    and reaches out to me.
Even when they sit and stare into nothingness,
    I know that you have knitted them in the womb
    and made them a person,
    and nothing can ever take away their personhood.
Search me, O God, and know my heart.
This experience tests my faith,
    but you will sustain me in my weariness;
You will help me get through this terrible time.
Help me to love my loved one with your love
    and to hold their hands and stay with them
    until they rest safely in your embrace.

© 2008 Richard L. Morgan and Jane Marie Thibault

Appendix 3

LEADING A SUPPORT GROUP FOR PERSONS WITH DEMENTIA

Procedure

1. Activity directors and volunteers may lead the group.

2. Activity director: Select eight to ten residents for the group, relying on the counsel of the nursing staff and/or chaplain as to who is appropriate for a group.

3. The group meets for an hour once a week.

4. Activity director: Use whatever resource you decide is most appropriate for the group. The suggestions in this appendix come from more than five years of working with support groups and creating a community that centers on cognitive stimulation, group interaction, and acceptance of everyone.

5. Begin with group-building and simple exercises to stimulate memory and interaction in each group.

6. Whenever someone new joins the group, make him or her feel welcome.

Community Building

1. In the first meeting or two, members may be anxious

or confused about the group's purpose. Reassure them that this will be a good experience.

2. Go around the table and ask each group member to say his or her name.

3. Leader: Ask each group member to say his or her name and then repeat the names of other group members. (This is an example of cherishing the moment; by the time the group meets again, names are forgotten and this exercise must be repeated.)

Suggested Activities

1. Trigger memory through nursery rhymes and proverbs.

Most group members will be able to recall nursery rhymes and proverbs. Leader: Say the first line of a nursery rhyme and ask the group to complete the rhyme. For example:

- Mary had a little lamb . . .
- Little Boy Blue, come blow your horn . . .
- Old Mother Hubbard went to the cupboard . . .
- You can lead a horse to water . . .
- An apple a day . . .
- A bird in the hand . . .
- A soft answer . . .

See Charles I. Kelly and Lawrence E. Kelly, "Commonly-Used Proverbs," on this Web site:

www.manythings.org/proverbs. Also visit these sites:

www.oneliners-and-proverbs.com

www.corsinet.com

www.creativeproverbs.com

2. Listen to old radio programs.

Play recordings of radio programs from the 1930s and 1940s, for example: *The Shadow, Little Orphan Annie, Stella Dallas, Lorenzo Jones,* and so on.

3. Recall poetry.

Read poems the group may have studied in high school, such as: Walt Whitman, "O Captain! My Captain!"; Joyce Kilmer, "Trees"; John Masefield, "Sea-Fever"; Henry Wadsworth Longfellow, "The Song of Hiawatha."

4. Reminisce through music.

Play recordings of familiar songs from the 1930s and 1940s, such as: "Night and Day" (1932), "Embraceable You" (1930), "The Way You Look Tonight" (1936), "You Are My Sunshine" (1940). See *16 Most Requested Songs of the 1940s,* vols. 1 and 2.

5. Create a story.

Use *LifeBio Memory Journal* (www.lifebio.com) and photographs to create stories.

6. Enjoy some humor.

Read good jokes to the group, and see if anyone can

remember a joke. See *The Mammoth Book of Jokes* (available at www.amazon.com) or see www.rd.com/alljokes.

7. Invite a young person to visit a session and read a story to the group.

Examples: *The Bobbsey Twins, Heidi, Rebecca of Sunnybrook Farm,* and *The Secret Garden.*

8. Share life stories.

Ask each group member if they would like to have their story recorded and given to their families. Secure permission from each person. Schedule a one-on-one interview, and record the person's story by writing it down or using a tape recorder. Fill gaps in their stories by talking with their families. Transcribe these stories and give written stories or recorded tapes to families.

Suggested resources: Beth Sanders, *LifeBio Memory Journal* (see www.lifebio.com) or Richard L. Morgan, *Remembering Your Story* (Upper Room Books, 2002).

9. Try some Montessori-based activities.

Montessori-based activities for persons with dementia can help them maintain or improve skills needed in their daily lives. The secret to the success of these activities is that they are open-ended so individuals gain a sense of accomplishment at any level of participation. See Cameron J. Camp, ed., *Montessori-Based Activities for Persons with Dementia,* vol. 1 (Towson, MD: Health Professions Press, 1999) and vol. 2 (2006).

Appendix 4

WORSHIP THROUGH MUSIC AND SYMBOLS

1. Show a picture of a sparrow and sing "His Eye Is on the Sparrow."
2. Display a picture of Jesus blessing the children and sing "Jesus Loves Me."
3. Wear dark sunglasses and then regular glasses as you sing "Open My Eyes, That I May See."
4. Show a cross and sing "The Old Rugged Cross."
5. Take a piece of string and place it around the group, as you sing "Blest Be the Tie That Binds."
6. Use a carving or photo of an old sea captain or a lighthouse and sing "Love Lifted Me," or "Let the Lower Lights Be Burning."
7. Show the group rosary beads and a clock. Then sing "Take Time to Be Holy."
8. Display a large Bible and sing "The B-i-b-l-e."
9. Light a small candle and sing "This Little Light of Mine."
10. Make a sign or poster of Psalm 119:105, KJV: "Thy Word is a lamp unto my feet, and a light unto my path." Shine a flashlight on the floor, and then walk a few steps as you explain that the Bible shows us where we are and lights our path so we know where to go.

For a more formal liturgy of worship services for people with Alzheimer's disease and their families, see *Worship Services for People with Alzheimer's Disease and Their Families: A Handbook,* compiled by Elizabeth Pohlmann and available from Eddy Alzheimer's Services, Marjorie Doyle Rockwell Center, 421 West Columbia St., Cohoes, NY 12047.

For an interfaith worship service for families of persons with Alzheimer's disease, write Waco Regional Office of the Alzheimer's Association, 6605 Sanger Avenue, Suite 1, Waco, TX 76710, or contact the Center for Gerontological Studies at Baylor University (www.baylor.edu).

NOTES

Introduction

1. Peter J. Whitehouse with Daniel George, *The Myth of Alzheimer's: What You Aren't Being Told about Today's Most Dreaded Diagnosis* (New York: St. Martin's Press, 2008), 8.

Chapter 2

1. From Dylan Thomas's poem "Do Not Go Gentle into That Good Night."

Chapter 3

1. David O. Moberg, "Spiritual Well-Being: Background [and] Issues" (Washington, DC: White House Conference on Aging, 1971), 3.

Chapter 5

1. Terry D. Hargrave, *Loving Your Parents When They Can No Longer Love You* (Grand Rapids, MI: Zondervan, 2005), 155.

Chapter 6

1. Joseph Scriven, "What a Friend We Have in Jesus," in *The United Methodist Hymnal* (Nashville: The United Methodist Publishing House, 1989), no. 526.

2. Katherine Hankey, "Tell Me the Old, Old Story," http://www.oremus.org/hymnal/t/t032.html (accessed January 29, 2009).

Chapter 7

1. From "The Passionate Pilgrim," in *The Works of William Shakespeare* (Roslyn, NY: Black's Readers Service, 1972), 1275.

2. See Richard H. Gentzler Jr., *Aging and Ministry in the 21st Century: An Inquiry Approach* (Nashville: Discipleship Resources, 2008), 26. Jane and I (Richard Morgan) urge congregations and pastors to use this excellent resource for initiating and maintaining a vital ministry for older adults in the parish.

3. *Now Is the Time: The Church's Challenge for Older Adult Ministry* (Princeton, NJ: Princeton Theological Seminary, 2007), 9–10.

4. Ibid., 1.

5. Ibid.

6. Henry Simmons, letter to Richard Morgan, June 8, 2008.

7. Stephen Sapp, letter to Richard Morgan, June 4, 2008.

8. Rick Gentzler, letter to Richard Morgan, June 10, 2008.

INDEX

ABOUT THE AUTHORS

Jane Marie Thibault is a gerontologist and clinical professor of Family and Geriatric Medicine at the University of Louisville School of Medicine, where she directs the geriatric evaluation and treatment program. Jane serves as chair of the Kentucky Institute for Aging and is a member of the Aging Committee for the Kentucky Conference of The United Methodist Church. A trained spiritual director, she is the author of *10 Gospel Promises for Later Life* and *A Deepening Love Affair: The Gift of God in Later Life.*

Richard L. Morgan holds three degrees from Union Theological Seminary in Richmond, Virginia, including a PhD in early Christian history and a master's degree in counseling from Wake Forest University; as well as an undergraduate degree from Davidson College. A retired chaplain and professor, Richard is the author of fourteen books, including *Settling In: My First Year in a Retirement Community* and *Remembering Your Story: Creating Your Own Spiritual Autobiography.* For more information, visit Richard's Web site: www.richardmorganauthor.com.